A MANUAL OF KEY BUDDHIST TERMS

A Categorization of Buddhist Terminology with Commentary

by

LOTSAWA KABA PALTSEG

Translated by

Thubten K. Rikey
and
Andrew Ruskin

LIBRARY OF TIBETAN WORKS AND ARCHIVES

ISBN: 81-85102-82-1

Published by the Library of Tibetan Works and Archives, Dharamsala, H.P., India, and printed at Indraprastha Press (CBT), 4 Bahadurshah Zafar Marg, New Delhi-110002.

CONTENTS

PUBLISHER'S NOTE

A Manual of Key Buddhist Terms, composed by the 8th-century Tibetan translator Lotsawa Kaba Paltseg, provides a lists of key Buddhist terms with useful commentaries.

The text deals precisely with such topics as the nature of the person; the method by which the individual relates to the world and the ensuing consequences; the law of dependent origination; the nature of emptiness; the path to Buddhahood from two different angles; various qualities of beings not yet freed from cyclic existence (samsara), etc.

We are happy to be bringing out this second edition of *A Manual of Key Buddhist Terms,* and are hopeful that this handy booklet will continue to be of use to students and scholars of Buddhism as a ready reference.

Thupten Rikey and Andrew Ruskin are to be complimented on their efforts in translating this valuable text.

Gyatsho Tshering
Director

INTRODUCTION

According to Buddhism, the universe is the co-creation of all beings. Furthermore, it is said that every living being inevitably arises out of a multitude of causes and conditions, and it is one's own actions that determine one's future. To have proper control over one's actions so as to make them result in a positive outcome, one needs to know how an action causes results according to karmic laws. In order to help sentient beings attain these positive, or virtuous, outcomes, which are antithetical to negative outcomes, or suffering, the Buddha gave his teachings. The author of the present text apparently had the same goal in mind when writing this enumeration. By clearly categorizing many key Buddhist terms, the author provides the reader with lists that are easy to memorize. With this knowledge one can develop one's practice, which makes the individual focus on the accumulation of virtue instead of negativity. Of course, many present-day practitioners do not feel it necessary to go so far as to memorize all the relevant terminology. However, since the author also supplies a commentary on the terms, the reader learns a lot about the world of Buddhism, its psychology and its philosophical outlook by studying the terms and their definitions.

STRUCTURE OF THE TEXT

The text can be roughly divided into eight topics. Parts 1 to 4 deal mostly with the nature, identity and mind of the person. The way these personal factors, or "dharmas", are categorized in the present work is similar to the system laid out by Arya Asanga in the *Abhidharmasamuccaya*[1] in the 5th century. This text later became the basis of the Mind Only school.

In the next section of the text, parts 5 to 8, the author discusses the method through which the individual relates to his or her world, and the ensuing consequences. Central to this are the 12 links of dependent arising, which cause suffering and bondage to cyclic existence.

The only way to free oneself from cyclic existence is to cut through the afflictive emotions, especially ignorance. Since ignorance creates all the other afflictive emotions, it is crucial to remove it by directly perceiving emptiness, which is ultimate truth.

Parts 9 to 12 are related to the nature of emptiness in contrast to relative truth.

Although directly perceiving emptiness is part of attaining Buddhahood, it is certainly not all that is necessary. Parts 15 to 18 illustrate the path to Buddhahood from two different angles. One approach is through the 37 practices which are methods of achieving enlightenment, and the other through the five paths of the Mahayana vehicle, along with the 10 perfections which are the practice, and the 10 Bodhisattva grounds which are their results, along with the ultimate result of Buddhahood.

It is far easier to attain a goal if one has a clear idea of the end result. With this in mind, parts 19 to 26 deal mostly with the surpassing characteristics of a Buddha. Not only do they help explain why one should have conviction in the Buddha and his teachings, they also show what every being can achieve, if he or she follows the Mahayana path to its conclusion.

Since Buddha was perfect, his teachings are invaluable. Yet, because they are so copious, they are hard to organize and understand. Therefore, parts 27 to 31 help to clarify points related to his teachings.

Although Buddha himself followed the Mahayana path, his teachings are often more in line with the Theravadin path. Parts 32 to 38 categorize various aspects of the paths of Hearers and Solitary Realizers. Whereas a Buddha has removed all obstructions to wisdom as well as all afflictive emotions, the Hearers and Solitary Realizers have only abandoned afflictive emotions. Thus they do not share many of the surpassing characteristics of a Buddha. Yet they are released from bondage to cyclic existence.

Part 39 to 44 enumerate various qualities of beings not yet freed from cyclic existence. Even birth in the form realm or formless realm does not guarantee that one will not fall back into the lower three realms again. The author briefly explains these states of mind stability meditation, which can be attained by practices common to Hinduism as well. This translation includes two works of an 8th-century scholar translator Kaba Paltseg.[2]

THE AUTHOR

As a translator, Kaba Paltseg was a genius and a recognised literary figure of his time. His outstanding translation ability and his good command of other literary skills as reflected in his works won him great admiration through the centuries. The 12th-century translator Ngog Loden Sherab recalled him in the following words:

> Variocana is like the sky
> Ka[ba Paltseg] and Chog are like the sun and moon.
> Rinchen Zangpo is like the morning star.
> Compared to them, I am simply a glow-worm.[3]

His contribution to the literary field consists of a number of translations and his own compositions—all to be found in the collections of Tibetan Buddhist canon. One of his most esteemed contributions is his catalogue of the translated scriptures, preserved in Tongthang Dhenkar Library in central Tibet.[4] No biography of him has so far come to light, and it is not known if one ever existed. However, an early 16th-century literary source[5] mentions him in the chapter on Padmasambhava's activities in Tibet, describing the role he played in promoting Buddhism in Tibet under the rule of King Trisong Detsen and his immediate successors, and connecting him with some of his period's historic events such as: the establishment of translating Buddhism into Tibetan at Samye; the invitation of Vimalamitra to Tibet; the reinstatement of Vairocana at Samye following his exile in Tshaba Rong; the contest of occult powers between Buddhists and Bonpos, and so forth. The authors of earlier sources, such as *sBa bzhad* and other annals, had made similar mention of these facts.

According to the present source, Kaba Paltseg was born to Kaba Loden and Drongza Dhocham of Kaba clan in Phan region in central Tibet. He and several other young Tibetans, including Vairocana and Chogro Luyi Gyaltshan, were summoned to Trisong Detsen's court, and were commanded to study translating skills at Samye under Shantirakshita. He soon gained mastery over Sanskrit as well as Tibetan and became an extraordinarily talented translator of Buddhist scriptures. Padmasambhava predicted that he would be the reincarnation of an Indian siddha who had a karmic link to become a genius at translation. Before being appointed as the principal translator at Samye, he was given ordination and initiated into the teachings of the outer, inner and secret tantras. From then on he took an active part in all the phases of the translation activities at Samye, in which over 100 translators were engaged. Because of his reputation for masterly translations, Trisong Detsen appointed him as assistant to Shantirakshita in the task of editing all the translations of the first phase of translation activities at Samye.

Following this, Trisong Detsen deputed him, assisted by three others, to invite from Kashmir a pandit who could check all those scriptures which were then translated into Tibetan. He returned from Kashmir with Vimalamitra, the most prominent pandit in Kashmir of that time, selecting him from among 500 others. He also acted as the principal mediator between Trisong Detsen and his anti-Buddhist ministers, who falsely accused Vairocana of having received impure teachings from India and exiled him to Tshaba Rong. After convincing the king to reinstate Vairocana at Samye, he and three others went to Tshaba Rong and brought Vairocana back to commence the second phase of translation activities. In the later part of his life, he did tantric practices and accordingly trained himself in numerous rites. At the time when the 25 Tibetan siddhas (*rje 'bangs nyer lnga*) held a contest of powers with Bonpo priests, he challenged and defeated his Bonpo counterpart, Tsemi Yungdrung. He was also among the leading figures who officiated at the funeral rites of Trisong Detsen.

The present source makes no mention of his date of death, but it is certain that he lived for a long time after the passing away of Trisong Detsen, since it was in the reign of Tride Songtsan—the next-to-immediate successor of Tri Songtsan—that he composed the catalogue.

TRANSLATION

Since English does not seem to be as perfect a vessel for the Dharma as Tibetan, there are many places within the text where the true meaning of the original does not exactly shine through. Fortunately, there have been many pioneers in the translation of Tibetan into English. We have therefore made extensive use of terms already created by others. By using somewhat standardized terms, we hope to avoid confusion. The main texts we used are *A Tibetan-English Dictionary of Buddhist Terminology*[6] and *Meditation on Emptiness*.[7] We also used *Meditative States*[8] for some terms related to the form and formless realms. When there was a conflict in translation, we chose the one that corresponded most closely with the commentary. Sometimes we had to use an entirely new term in order to make it consistent with the commentary. Also, there were a couple of occasions when we could not find any previous translation. In those cases, with the assistance of Geshe Sonam Rinchen, we devised our own terms. We greatly appreciate Geshe Sonam Rinchen's help, and we hope that the understanding he sought to convey to us comes through in the translation. Also, we thank Mr. Richard Guard for editing the English translation.

Although the Tibetan scholars translated the Sanskrit texts so perfectly that the original can often be reconstructed from the Tibetan, there has been no such standardization of terms translated from Tibetan into English. Thus the reader should not be surprised to see the same Tibetan word with two or more English correlates in various sections of the text. However, we felt that different English terms were better suited to convey the meanings in different contexts. We apologize for any confusion that this might create.

After arriving at a suitable wording for the root text, we proceeded to translate the commentary. In translating the commentary, we used only the parts related directly to the root text. Many sections of the commentary remain untranslated. Furthermore, we remained faithful to the commentary's explanation of the terminology even when it conflicted with other definitions. Again, we hope this will enrich the reader's understandings of the terms and their range of meaning. For those who want to check the Tibetan terms against a different English translation, we have included the Tibetan text next to the English in the outline section. Since some students may use this text to improve their knowledge of Tibetan, we have decided to leave out the numbers in the Tibetan text, so as to avoid confusion with the terms themselves.

NOTES

1. Tengyur (Peking), Vol. 112, No: 550.
2. *Chos kyi rnam grangs* and *Chos kyi rnam grangs kyi brjed byang* (Peking Tenjur, No.5850 & 5849).
3. *Op.cit.* Khetsun Sangpo, *Biographical Dictionary of Tibet and Tibetan Buddhism*, Vol.III, p.83.
4. *sTong thang ldan dkar ru bka' dang bstan bcos 'gyur ro cog gi dkar chag* (Peking Tenjur No.5851).
5. *Pad ma thang yig*, Gangtok, 1977.
6. Tsepak Rigzin, *A Tibetan-English Dictionary of Buddhist Terminology*, published by the Library of Tibetan Works and Archives, Dharamsala, 1986.
7. Jeffrey Hopkins, *Meditation on Emptiness*, Wisdom Publications, London, 1985.
8. Leah Zahler and Jeffrey Hopkins, *Meditative States in Tibetan Buddhism*, Wisdom Publications, London, 1983.

A CATEGORIZATION OF BUDDHIST TERMINOLOGY

Homage to Manjushri.

1. THE FIVE AGGREGATES (ཕུང་པོ།)

A. THE 15 FORM AGGREGATES (གཟུགས་ཀྱི་ཕུང་པོ།)

1-4). *The four elements* (འབྱུང་བ།)

a. earth element (ས།)

b. water element (ཆུ།)

c. fire element (མེ།)

d. air element (རླུང་།)

5-15). *The physical manifestations stemming from the four elements* (འབྱུར་བྱས་པའི་གཟུགས།)

a. visual faculty (མིག་གི་དབང་པོ།)

b. auditory faculty (རྣའི་དབང་པོ།)

c. olfactory faculty (སྣའི་དབང་པོ།)

d. gustatory faculty (ལྕེའི་དབང་པོ།)

e. tactile faculty (ལུས་ཀྱི་དབང་པོ།)

f. form (གཟུགས།)

g. sound (སྒྲ།)

h. smell (དྲི།)

i. taste (རོ།)

j. tangible objects (རེག་བྱ།)

k. intangible objects (རྣམ་པར་རིག་བྱེད་མ་ཡིན་པ།)

It is through the combination and permutations of the four elements that the body, its sense organs, and even the objects of the sense organs arise.

B. The Three Feeling Aggregates (ཚོར་བའི་དབང་པོ།)

1) happiness (བདེ་བ།)

2) suffering (སྡུག་བསྔལ་བ།)

3) neutral (གཉིས་ཀ་མ་ཡིན་པ།)

A feeling is a state which has no form or consciousness. When a feeling of *happiness* arises, one wants it to remain. When it disappears, one wants it to return. *Suffering*, which causes harm to body or mind, is a state that one never wants to meet. One neither wants nor does not want a *neutral* state. This is because the neutral state neither brings happiness nor suffering to the body or mind.

C. The Three Recognition Aggregates (འདུ་ཤེས་ཀྱིས་ཕུང་པོ།)

1) small (ཆུང་དུ།)

2) extensive (རྒྱ་ཆེན་པོ།)

3) limitless (ཚད་མེད་པ།)

The *recognition aggregate* is that aggregate which distinguishes characteristics such as shape and color in sense objects such as sound and form. The *small recognition aggregate* recognizes objects in the desire realm. The *extensive recognition aggregate* recognizes objects in the form realm. The *limitless recognition aggregate* recognizes objects in the formless realm.

D. Aggregate of Compositional Factors

(འདུ་བྱེད་ཀྱི་ཕུང་པོ།)

The *aggregate of compositional factors* comprises the mental factors which are not part of the feeling aggregate nor of the recognition aggregate; rather, they are the conglomeration of many causes and conditions. (This aggregate has also been rendered into English as impulse, volition, etc. Compositional factors is the most literal of the translation.)

1) *Fifty-one psychic factors* (སེམས་ལས་བྱུང་བ།)

a) omnipresent factors (ཀུན་འགྲོ་ལྔ།)

   i) contact (རེག་པ།)

   ii) mental engagement (ཡིད་ལ་བྱེད་པ།)

   iii) feeling (ཚོར་བ།)

   iv) recognition (འདུ་ཤེས།)

   v) intention (སེམས་པ།)

The *omnipresent factors* are present in virtuous, non-virtuous and neutral states. *Contact* comprises the sense object, the sense organ, and the sense consciousness. When the sense consciousness perceives an object through the sense organ, then a feeling such as happiness arises. *Mental engagement* is the penetration of the mind into the object through attention. As a result of the ripening of virtuous, non-virtuous and neutral karma, one experiences happiness, suffering, or a neutral state respectively. This is called *feeling*. *Recognition* means the act of distinguishing characteristics of the objects of the five sense consiousnesses. *Intention* is the mental factor which draws the mind to virtuous, non-virtuous or neutral [objects, which thus produce virtuous, non-virtuous, or neutral] states of mind. It operates similarly to a magnet which draws a pin in various directions.

b) determining factors (ཡུལ་སོ་སོར་ངེས་པ།)

   i) aspiration (འདུན་པ།)

   ii) belief (མོས་པ།)

   iii) mindfulness (དྲན་པ།)

   iv) stabilization (ཏིང་ངེ་འཛིན།)

   v) knowledge (ཤེས་རབ།)

Unlike the omnipresent factors, which arise whenever any virtuous, non-virtuous or neutral stimulus exists, the *determining factors* only occur in relation to certain stimuli. Thus one's aspiration, for

4 A Manual of Key Buddhist Terms

example, only arises in response to certain objects, unlike the omnipresent factors which arise in response to any object. *Aspiration* is the desire that arises when the sense organ and sense consciousness penetrate an object, regardless of the nature of that object. *Belief* is the holding of a specific object of discernment to be known exactly as it is. Yet only objects in which one has belief are discerned, and no others. One uses direct and inferential perception to examine the object, and thus discernment can remove doubt and increase conviction in the teachings of the sutras and commentaries. Or discernment can be the holding of the view that a fundamental characteristic of all phenomena is impermanence as opposed to permanence and bliss. In this way, belief in these views arises. *Mindfulness* means that one does not forget the object with which one has become familiar over a long period of time. Thus the object remains clear in the mind as if one is conjuring up an image through referring to it in conversation. [For example, we think of a dog when someone says 'dog']. *Stabilization* means that one focuses single-pointedly on the object of investigation. The object of investigation is the object upon which one bases one's examination of ultimate truth, that is, the lack of inherent existence and inherent production, or it is the object from which one gains insight into the four noble truths. *Single-pointedness* refers to the undistracted focus on the meditative object, just as one twists a thread to a fine point in order to put it through the eye of the needle. *Wisdom* can be divided into three categories. In applying belief and stabilization to an object, [first,] one uses reasoning and understands the ultimate nature of the object. [Second,] one follows the path of the [non-Buddhist] forders and, without using correct reasoning, comes to a mistaken notion of reality. The third type of individual either innately understands reality, or understands it very quickly upon hearing teachings on it.

c) virtuous factors (དགེ་བ།)

  i) faith (དད་པ།)

  ii) shame (ངོ་ཚ་ཤེས་པ།)

  iii) embarrassment (ཁྲེལ་ཡོད་པ།)

  iv) non-attachment (མ་ཆགས་པ།)

  v) non-hatred (ཞེ་སྡང་མེད་པ།)

vi) non-ignorance (གཏི་མུག་མེད་པ།)

vii) effort (བརྩོན་འགྲུས།)

viii) pliancy (ཤིན་ཏུ་སྦྱངས་པ།)

ix) conscientiousness (བག་ཡོད་པ།)

x) equanimity (བཏང་སྙོམས།)

xi) non-harmfulness (རྣམ་པར་མི་འཚེ་བ།)

The first of the virtuous factors is faith. *Faith* is a superior conviction in objects such as karma, the results of karma, and the four noble truths. It is also the pure thought that arises when one sees the virtuous qualities of the Three Jewels. *Shame* is the mental factor which causes one to refrain from various actions. A religious practitioner refrains from certain actions because of realizing that they are inappropriate for a religious practitioner to engage in; one avoids certain other actions because of realizing that they are inappropriate and will lead to a negative rebirth; and one refrains from certain types of speech out of fear that they are inappropriate and will cause one's own defamation. *Embarrassment* is the refraining from certain actions out of fear that they will lead to the decline of one's position amongst others. *Non-attachment* is the antidote to attachment. It arises when one realizes that one's body and wealth are impure, having the nature of aging, illness and death. Thus one's mind separates from these phenomena and does not grasp at them. The antidote to hatred is *non-hatred*, which is also love. The objects of hatred are enemies, poison and weapons. Hatred is the thought that destruction, harm or loss should befall one's enemies. The antidote to this is not allowing these thoughts or their implementation to arise, and developing love for one's enemies as if they were one's own cherished children. The *antidote to ignorance* is the realization that perfection is perfect. Ignorance is the conception that phenomena and beings are inherently existent, permanent, blissful, and pure. The antidotes to this wrong view are such conceptions as emptiness and selflessness, which are developed through wisdom, effort, stabilization, and familiarity. *Effort* is the antidote to laziness, in that one takes delight in virtuous actions. *Pliancy* is the antidote to wrongful abiding of body and mind. Wrongful abiding of the body is sleepiness and painful joints. Wrongful abiding of the mind is excitation and lethargy. Wrongful abiding leads to negative rebirths. The antidotes to these are lightness and peacefulness of body and single-pointedness of mind. *Conscientiousness* is the antidote to carelessness. Conscientiousness is the abiding in effort without attachment, anger or ignorance, which allows one to abandon non-virtuous actions. One applies the antidote to these through meditation on virtuous actions, which is familiarization with both mundane and transmundane virtuous activities. While one abides in this state without attachment, anger or ignorance through the application of effort, one develops a composure which prevents the recurrence of lethargy or excitement. Then finally one develops a spontaneous abiding in *equanimity* free of any possibility of lethargy or excitement recurring. In this way, it becomes impossible for attachment and other afflictive emotions to arise. *Non-harmfulness* is the antidote to harmfulness. Harmfulness comprises actions such as killing , agitating, threatening or scolding others. If one has the antidote, compassion, one will not even think of hurting others.

d) six root afflictions (རྩ་ཉོན།)

    i) desire (འདོད་ཆགས།)

    ii) anger (ཁོང་ཁྲོ།)

    iii) pride (ང་རྒྱལ།)

        a) pride (ང་རྒྱལ།)

        b) excessive pride (ཆེ་བའི་ང་རྒྱལ།)

        c) pride beyond pride (ང་རྒྱལ་ལས་ཀྱང་ང་རྒྱལ།)

        d) pride of thinking 'I' (ངའི་སྙམ་པའི་ང་རྒྱལ།)

        e) pride of conceit (མངོན་པའི་ང་རྒྱལ།)

        f) pride of slight inferiority (ཅུང་ཟད་སྙམ་པའི་ང་རྒྱལ།)

        g) wrongful pride (ལོག་པའི་ང་རྒྱལ།)

    iv) ignorance (མ་རིག་པ།)

    v) wrong view (ལྟ་བ།)

        a) view of the transitory collection (འཇིག་ཚོགས་ལ་ལྟ་བ།)

        b) view holding to an extreme (མཐར་འཛིན་པའི་ལྟ་བ།)

        c) perverse view (ལོག་པར་ལྟ་བ།)

d) conception of a (wrong) view as supreme (ལྟ་བ་མཆོག་ཏུ་ འཛིན་པ།)

e) conception of (bad) ethics and modes of conduct as supreme (ཚུལ་ཁྲིམས་དང་བརྟུལ་ཞུགས་མཆོག་ཏུ་འཛིན་པ།)

vi) doubt (ཐེ་ཚོམ།)

Desire is the clinging and extraordinary attachment to the five corrupted aggregates. The corrupted aggregates are said to be corrupted because they originate from the corrupted causes of wrong wishes, wrong view, wrong conduct and the belief in self. Clinging is the inability to tolerate separation from the five aggregates. Extraordinary attachment is the wish to take rebirth in a body possessing the five corrupted aggregates. In the same way, after an oil stain becomes set in clothing, it becomes very difficult to remove. *Anger* is the motivation to harm sentient beings. One contemplates hurting others, such as one's enemies, through actions such as threatening or killing. Naturally, this thought can only lead to suffering and cannot result in peace. *Pride* is the distinction between self and others that arises due to the misconception of an inherently existing self, which leads to a lack of respect and to haughtiness. The *pride of pride* is the inflation of self that comes from the perception that one's skills, appearance, class, wealth and so forth are better than others'. *Excessive pride* is the belief that one is superior to another in terms of conduct and so forth, even though one's qualities are equal to another's. *Pride beyond pride* is the belief that one is superior even to those who are superior to oneself. The *pride of thinking* 'I' is the misconception that the self and the possessions of self exist inherently. The *pride of conceit* is the thought that one has become a Superior, or Arya, even though one has only made small achievements and has neither attained stabilization nor the rank of Arya. The *pride of slight inferiority* is the belief that one is slightly lower than those who are much higher than oneself. *Wrongful pride* is the haughtiness which accompanies the view that one has attained virtuous qualities, whereas one actually has various faults and has accomplished nothing. *Ignorance* is the lack of knowledge with respect to karma, the results of karma, the truths, and the Three Jewels. It is also falling under the influence of one's innate beliefs and of wrong schools of thought. Of the five types of wrong view, the first is the *view of the transitory collection*. The five aggregates are subject to momentary impermanence, and they are the conglomeration of many constituents. Thus this wrong view conceives of an unproduced self and possessions of the self, which do not actually exist. The *view holding to an extreme* consists of eternalism or nihilism. Some believe that like a snake's skin, one casts off one life and takes another. Others believe that, like a fire which has used up all of its wood, a person dies, and there is no remainder. *Perverse view* is a lack of respect and a denial of karma, the fruits of karma, the truths, the Three Jewels, cyclic existence, rebirth and so forth. The *conception of wrong views as supreme* is the belief that the three previously stated wrong views and the belief in the beneficial nature of one's body and circumstances are supreme. One thinks that these views are to be held as important, and that no other views are superior to these views. The *conception of bad ethics and modes of conduct as supreme* consists of the belief that the ethics of abandoning the seven faults through undergoing hardships, the imitation of dogs and cows, allowing one's hair to become matted and so forth will lead to liberation. *Doubt* is when one simultaneously entertains two points of view regarding the truths and so forth. One questions whether or not karma, the results of karma, the truths and the Three Jewels exist. If they do exist, one questions whether or not they have virtuous qualities. In this way, the mind goes in two different directions.

e) secondary afflictions (ཉེ་བའི་ཉོན་མོངས་པ།)

   i) belligerence (ཁྲོ་བ།)

   ii) resentment (འཁོན་དུ་འཛིན་པ།)

   iii) concealment (འཆབ་པ།)

   iv) spite (འཚིག་པ།)

   v) jealousy (ཕྲག་དོག)

   vi) miserliness (སེར་སྣ།)

   vii) dissimulation (གཡོ།)

  viii) deceit (སྒྱུ།)

   ix) haughtiness (རྒྱགས་པ།)

   x) harmfulness (རྣམ་པར་འཚེ་བ།)

   xi) non-shame (ངོ་ཚ་མེད་པ།)

xii) non-embarrassment (ཁྲེལ་མེད་པ།)

xiii) lethargy (རྨུགས་པ།)

xiv) excitement (རྒོད་པ།)

xv) non-faith (མ་དད་པ།)

xvi) laziness (ལེ་ལོ།)

xvii) non-conscientiousness (བག་མེད་པ།)

xviii) forgetfulness (བརྗེད་ངེས་པ།)

xix) non-introspection (ཤེས་བཞིན་མ་ཡིན་པ།)

xx) distraction (རྣམ་པར་གཡེང་བ།)

Belligerence is the intention to harm a being in one's immediate environment. Enemies from the past and future are not included; only those who are directly visible are objects of belligerence. *Resentment* is compared to a knot, in that it doesn't unravel. One refuses to let go of the harmful intention to eventually hurt someone such as an enemy who has hurt oneself or those who are close to one. *Concealment* is hiding one's inappropriate actions. After committing a non-virtuous action, one should confess one's negativities to a spiritual guide who will point out the faults of the action. Yet, instead, one claims that one has no faults. *Spite* is when one uses harsh words to point out another person's faults, thus causing the other person to be unhappy. *Jealousy* is when one becomes profoundly disturbed by other people's good fortune. After one sees another's qualities such as wealth , respect, learning or conduct, one develops intolerable anger through the power of attachment. *Miserliness* is an attitude not conducive with generosity, through which one holds onto all one's possessions because of attachment to them. Through the increase of desire, one becomes so attached to the objects one needs to survive that giving them away seems intolerable. One cannot even be generous to the Three Jewels or to beggars. One even becomes possessive in regards to one's rubbish.

   Dissimulation is the dishonesty that comes from trying to hide one's faults from others. Because one wants wealth and respect, one attempts to eradicate any harm to one's reputation whenever one suspects that others have recognized one's faults. *Deceit* is fooling others and leading them to impure purposes. In order to receive profit, respect and wealth, one pretends to have virtuous qualities that one does not have, or one performs magical tricks. *Haughtiness* is the belief that what one has is sufficient because one is extremely happy with this good fortune to which one is attached. Good fortune can be one's class, friends, wealth, skills, appearance and so forth. Because one possesses these things, one becomes peaceful. Thus with an easy mind, one searches for nothing else, and one does not practise religion. *Harmfulness* is the abuse of others through various physical actions such as slapping or striking, due to lack of compassion. *Non-shame* is the lack of refraining from inappropriate actions. These types of actions occur when one falls under the power of desire, hatred and ignorance. Inappropriate actions are those actions which are non- virtuous. It is a negativity when a brahmin, monk or yogi engages in non-virtuous acts because he doesn't consider them to be inappropriate. *Non-embarrassment* is the lack of refraining from certain non-virtuous acts because one is not afraid of the decline in one's position amongst others.

Lethargy is an inappropriate mental state that is a lack of clarity of the observed object. It results in inappropriate mental states during the time of listening to the teachings and contemplation through an increase of ignorance, which is due to a lack of superior, clear wisdom. *Excitement* is an unpacified state. Through the increase of attachment, one's mind becomes distracted, and it turns to previous unproductive behaviour. This then causes obstacles to meditation. *Non-faith* is the lack of conviction and faith in karma, the fruits of karma, the truths and the Three Jewels. It is not conducive to faith. Without faith, one does not undertake virtuous actions. *Laziness* means that one does not revel in virtuous activities. It is not conducive to effort. One does not engage in virtuous activities such as listening, contemplating and meditating on the teachings. One's merit declines through excessive sleep and reclining; through the increase of ignorance one does not exert effort in virtuous activities, and thus one does not take delight in them. *Non-conscientiousness* is the lack of protection of the mind from the afflictive emotions such as desire, hatred, ignorance and laziness. One does not meditate on virtuous actions. Desire, hatred and ignorance act as the cause of abiding in laziness. One does not protect the mind because one allows it to wander to these non-virtuous mental factors. One does not repeatedly meditate on virtuous thoughts such as non-attachment, and thus one does not become familiar with these ideas. *Forgetfulness* is attentiveness to afflictive emotions such as desire through familiarization with them, and one forgets the supreme teachings, which leads to the lack of clarity of virtuous objects. *Non-introspection* is the mixture of afflictive emotions with wisdom. *Distraction* is the wandering of the mind to sense objects through the increase of desire, hatred and ignorance. Thus one engages in activities of body, speech, and mind without regard to whether or not these activities are dictated by wisdom.

f) changeable factors (གཞན་དུ་འགྱུར་བ།)

   i) contrition (འགྱོད་པ།)

   ii) sleep (གཉིད།)

   iii) investigation (རྟོག་པ།)

   iv) analysis (དཔྱོད་པ།)

The *changeable factors* are inderterminate regarding whether they become virtuous or non-virtuous factors. They play a part in virtuous, non-virtuous, or neutral activities. They are called changeable factors because they change the mental state into a virtuous or non-virtuous one depending upon the direction they are going. *Contrition* is an impression left on the mind. Through the increase of contrition, one considers a virtuous, non-virtuous, or neutral past action, or the lack of such an action to be negative. Thus if one considers one's virtuous activities to be negative, this is non-virtuous. Contrition for both non-virtuous and neutral actions is considered to be virtuous. *Sleep* is the inability to stay engaged with external objects, so that the mind gathers within. Through torpor, heaviness of body, mental darkness and lethargy, one loses one's mental focus and physical capabilities. If sleep interrupts virtuous activities, it is non-virtuous. If sleep interrupts non-virtuous activities, then it is virtuous. If a neutral activity is interrupted, then the sleep is neutral. Also the contents of one's dreams can lead to virtue, non-virtue, or neutrality. *Investigation* is attentiveness by consciousness to any object of examination. One examines roughly whatever the particular object of consciousness is. For instance, it is the identification of a pot as a pot or a piece of cloth as a piece of cloth. *Analysis* is a detailed examination of the object of investigation to which one has attentiveness. In the example above, one does not just identify the pot, but one ascertains in detail its quality, color and shape.

2) *Non-associated compositional factors*

(སེམས་དང་ལྡན་པ་མ་ཡིན་པ།)

[These are factors attributed to processes that occur to the body, mind and mental factors.]

a) acquisition (ཐོབ་པ།)

b) absorption without discrimination (འདུ་ཤེས་མེད་པའི་འགོག་པ་ལ་ སྙོམས་པར་འཇུག་པ།)

c) absorption of cessation (འགོག་པའི་སྙོམས་པར་འཇུག་པ།)

d) one having no discrimination (འདུ་ཤེས་མེད་པ།)

e) life faculty (སྲོག་གི་དབང་པོ།)

f) similarity of type (རིགས་མཐུན་པ།)

g) birth (སྐྱེ་བ།)

h) aging (རྒ་བ།)

i) duration (གནས་པ།)

j) impermanence (མི་རྟག་པ།)

k) group of stems (མིང་གི་ཚོགས།)

l) group of words (ཚིག་གི་ཚོགས།)

m) group of letters (ཡི་གེའི་ཚོགས།)

n) state of an ordinary being (སོ་སོའི་སྐྱེ་བོ་ཉིད།)

Non-associated compositional factors are said to be non-associated because they exist even at times when the mind is not operating, such as non-discriminatory states, states of meditative cessation, fainting and deep sleep. *Acquisition* is the accumulation of new impressions on one's mental continuum that result from virtuous, non-virtuous and neutral activities. Then they remain there from that point onward. *Absorption without discrimination* is the cessation of an unstable mind and unstable mental factors through the attainment of the fourth concentration after one wrongly identifies it as passing beyond the nature of suffering. Thus it is unlike the states preceding it. It is free from faults such as desire which are present in all the states which precede the fourth concentration. In order to attain the stage of 'great fruit', the highest stage of the fourth concentration, one must extirpate the six consciousnesses and their accompanying discriminations. The *absorption of cessation* is a state free from the afflictive emotions such as the desire for even the state of perception of nothingness. One even goes beyond the peak of cyclic existence. Through the appearance to the mind of the aspiration to attain this state identified as complete pacification, one extirpates the instabilities of the mind and mental factors. Also, one extirpates those enduring factors such as afflicted consciousness. *Having no discrimination* is the result of absorption without discrimination. After one is born amongst the deities without discrimination, one extirpates the instabilities of the mind and mental factors. As a result of absorption without discrimination, one is born on the level of 'great fruit'. At first, one has discrimination. As a result of one's previous efforts, one's discrimination becomes ever more subtle until it is finally eradicated. Then one has extraordinary concentration. All of the six consciousnesses have been extirpated. The *life faculty* is that which stays with one throughout the length of one's life. This length, which can be anywhere from a thousand years to a single moment, is in accordance with one's species, such as that of a god or a fly, and is determined by karma. *Similarity of type* is the shape of body which is appropriate to one's species, such as that of a human, god or animal. *Birth* is the production of that which did not exist before, in accordance with one's species, such as that of a human or deity. Arising from birth, *aging* is the continuous change of an individual into something new. Aging is the change that occurs to the five aggregates starting with the first moment in the womb and continuing until one has grey hair and wrinkles. *Duration* is the continuum which flows through the continuity of changing moments. After the produced aggregates arise, then the continuum abides in the continuous sequence of moments until death. *Impermanence* is the cessation of this continuous sequence of moments within one's continuum. After the continuous sequence of moments of the aggregates ceases, one becomes separated from one's life, and the aggregates are abolished. The *group of stems* is the arbitrary attachment of sounds to the nature of phenomena. By creating different sounds for different phenomena, one creates names for them, which are then understood. For instance, fire and water are called 'agni' and 'pani' in Sanskrit, yet the meaning is the same [in any language]. It is implicitly understood that fire burns and water flows, or one can think that words are the conglomeration of many syllables, which then gives a word its meaning. In terms of the arbitrary attachment of sounds to the nature of phenomena, one attaches the arbitrary sounds of 'fire' and 'water' to the phenomena whose natures are heat and flowing respectively. If it were not just an arbitrary sound but were the actual phenomenon, one's mouth would burn when one said 'fire'. The *group of words* is the attachment of words composed of arbitrary sounds to the specific nature of phenomena. For instance, water is impermanent, suffering, empty of inherent existence, and selfless. One can apply this type of characterization to all phenomena. The purpose of the *group of letters* is the clarification of the group of stems and the group of words. The collection of the prototypes of many letters such as "A" and "B" creates the group of letters. The *state of an ordinary being* is the state of one who has not attained the path of an Arya. One has not abandoned afflictive emotions such as desire, and under the power of karma one takes on various types of rebirths. An Arya is any Stream-enterer or anyone on the first [Bodhisattva] ground or higher. The path of an Arya is the abandoning of the obscurations of the path of seeing and the path of accumulation. If one does not accomplish this state, one must continually take rebirths.

E. The Consciousness Aggregates (རྣམ་པར་ཤེས་པ།)

1) eye consciousness (མིག་གི་རྣམ་པར་ཤེས་པ།)

2) ear consciousness (རྣ་བའི་རྣམ་པར་ཤེས་པ།)

3) nose consciousness (སྣའི་རྣམ་པར་ཤེས་པ།)

4) tongue consciousness (ལྕེའི་རྣམ་པར་ཤེས་པ།)

5) body consciousness (ལུས་ཀྱི་རྣམ་པར་ཤེས་པ།)

6) mental consciousness (ཡིད་ཀྱི་རྣམ་པར་ཤེས་པ།)

7) afflicted consciousness (ཉོན་མོངས་པ་ཅན་གྱི་ཡིད།)

   a) obscuration with respect to a self (བདག་ཏུ་རྨོངས་པ།)

   b) view of a self (བདག་ཏུ་ལྟ་བ།)

   c) pride in a self (བདག་ཏུ་ང་རྒྱལ་བ།)

   d) attachment to a self (བདག་ཏུ་ཆགས་པ།)

8) Mind as basis of all (ཀུན་གཞི་རྣམ་པར་ཤེས་པ།)

   a) the only foundation for all (ས་བོན་ཐམས་ཅད་ཀྱི་གཞི་ཉིད།)

   b) the basis of all rebirth (ལུས་ཀྱི་ཀུན་གཞི།)

   c) the cause of all rebirth (རྒྱུ་ཉིད།)

   d) it dwells only within the body (ལུས་ལ་གནས་པ་ཉིད།)

   e) no recognition of distinct objects and their characteristics
     (དམིགས་པ་དང་རྣམ་པ་ཡོངས་སུ་མ་ཆད་པ།)

   f) impartiality (རིས་གཅིག་པ།)

   g) unchanging receptivity (རྒྱུན་ཆགས་པར་འཇུག་པ།)

Consciousness is the perception of an object. Each of the eight consciousnesses perceives its own specific type of object. (The mental faculty, or mind sense power, is the moment of cessation of the six consciousnesses.)

2. THE EIGHT OBJECTS (ཡུལ།)

a. feelings (ཚོར་བ།)

b. recognitions (འདུ་ཤེས།)

c. composite factors (འདུ་བྱེད།)

d. intangible objects (རྣམ་པར་རིག་བྱེད་མ་ཡིན་པ།)

e. unproduced space (འདུ་མ་བྱས་ནམ་མཁའ།)

f. non-analytical cessation (སོ་སོར་བརྟགས་པ་མ་ཡིན་པའི་འགོག་པ།)

g. analytical cessation (སོ་སོར་བརྟགས་འགོག་)

h. suchness (དེ་བཞིན་ཉིད།)

3. THE 12 SOURCES (སྐྱེ་མཆེད།)

a. eye sense power (མིག་གི་སྐྱེ་མཆེད།)

b. ear sense power (རྣའི་སྐྱེ་མཆེད།)

c. nose sense power (སྣའི་སྐྱེ་མཆེད།)

d. tongue sense power (ལྕེའི་སྐྱེ་མཆེད།)

e. body sense power (ལུས་ཀྱི་སྐྱེ་མཆེད།)

f. mind sense power (ཡིད་ཀྱི་སྐྱེ་མཆེད།)

g. form (གཟུགས་ཀྱི་སྐྱེ་མཆེད།)

h. sound (སྒྲའི་སྐྱེ་མཆེད།)

i. odor (དྲིའི་སྐྱེ་མཆེད།)

j. taste (རོ་ཡི་སྐྱེ་མཆེད།)

k. tangible object (རེག་བྱའི་སྐྱེ་མཆེད།)

l. phenomenon (ཆོས་ཀྱི་སྐྱེད་མཆེད།)

The 12 sources are either the causes or the doors by which the consciousnesses arise. All the eight consciousnesses that are included in the consciousness aggregate are considered to be part of the mind sense power. The eight objects are sources which are included under the category of phenomena.

4. THE 18 CONSTITUENTS (ཁམས།)

a. eye sense power (མིག་གི་ཁམས།)

b. form (གཟུགས་ཀྱི་ཁམས།)

c. eye consciousness (མིག་གི་རྣམ་པར་ཤེས་པའི་ཁམས།)

d. ear sense power (རྣའི་ཁམས།)

e. sound (སྒྲའི་ཁམས།)

f. ear consciousness (རྣ་བའི་རྣམ་པར་ཤེས་པའི་ཁམས།)

g. nose sense power (སྣའི་ཁམས།)

h. odor (དྲིའི་ཁམས།)

i. nose consciousness (སྣའི་རྣམ་པར་ཤེས་པའི་ཁམས།)

j. tongue sense power (ལྕེའི་ཁམས།)

k. taste (རོའི་ཁམས།)

l. body sense power (ལུས་ཀྱི་ཁམས།)

m. tangible objects (རེག་བྱ།)

n. body consciousness (ལུས་ཀྱི་རྣམ་པར་ཤེས་པའི་ཁམས།)

o. tongue consciousness (ལྕེའི་རྣམ་པར་ཤེས་པའི་ཁམས།)

p. mind sense power (ཡིད་ཀྱི་ཁམས།)

q. phenomenon (ཆོས་ཀྱི་ཁམས།)

r. mental consciousness (ཡིད་ཀྱི་རྣམ་པར་ཤེས་པའི་ཁམས།)

The 18 constituents consist of the six sense objects, six sense powers, and six consciousnesses. As an example of why one calls consciousness a constituent, one can think of the mind basis-of-all as a constituent of the arising of names and forms. Also, it is the seed of the arising of internal phenomena.

5. DEPENDENT ARISING (རྟེན་འབྲེལ།)

A. THE LINKS OF EXTERNAL DEPENDENT ARISING
(ཕྱི་རྟེན་ཅིང་འབྲེལ་བ།)

1) seed (ས་བོན།)

2) sprout (མྱུ་གུ།)

3) petal (འདབ་མ།)

4) trunk (སྡོང་བུ།)

5) bud (སྦུ་གུ།)

6) pith (སྙིང་པོ།)

7) flower (མེ་ཏོག)

8) fruit (འབྲས་བུ།)

B. THE SIX CAUSES OF EXTERNAL DEPENDENT ARISING
(རྒྱུ་ན།)

1) earth (ས།)

2) water (ཆུ།)

3) fire (མེ།)

4) air (རླུང་།)

5) space (ནམ་མཁའ།)

6) time (དུས།)

C. THE 12 LINKS OF INTERNAL DEPENDENT ARISING
(ནང་གི་རྟེན་ཅིང་འབྲེལ་བ།)

[These only become the accumulation of suffering.]

1) ignorance (མ་རིག་པ།)

2) action (འདུ་བྱེད།)

3) consciousness (རྣམ་པར་ཤེས་པ།)

4) name and form (མིང་དང་གཟུགས།)

5) six sources (སྐྱེ་མཆེད་དྲུག་)

6) contact (རེག་པ།)

7) feeling (ཚོར་བ།)

8) attachment (སྲིད་པ།)

9) grasping (ལེན་པ།)

10) existence (སྲིད་པ།)

11) birth (སྐྱེ་བ།)

12) aging (རྒ་བ།), death (ཤི།), mourning (སྐྱོ་ངན།), lamentation (སྨྲེ་ངག་འདོན་པ།), suffering (སྡུག་བསྔལ།), unhappiness (ཡིད་མི་བདེ་བ།) and agitation (འཁྲུགས་པ།)

The *12 links of internal dependent arising* are the way in which the causes of internal phenomena arise and then the way in which they bring results. *Ignorance* comes from great darkness. Similar to the way darkness obscures even the rough appearance of produced things, the darkness of mind obscures one's vision of the nature of karma, the results of karma, the truths, the qualities of the Three Jewels, and the emptiness of phenomena. Virtuous, non-virtuous or neutral karma produced in the three realms is called *action*. In order to perceive clearly, one has consciousness. All internal and external phenomena, such as forms and sounds, are objects perceived by a consciousness such as an eye *consciousness*. Once an object becomes known, this is called consciousness. In order to provide mutual support, there is both *name and form*. Like the poles which are the support of a tent, name and form mutually support each other. The doors of the arising of consciousness are the *six sources*. These sources act as a cause of the mind and the mental factors, and are also called the sense powers. *Contact* is the meeting of the sense object, the sense power, and the sense consciousness. *Feeling* is a result of experience. After the meeting of the sense object, the sense power and the sense consciousness, one experiences happiness or suffering depending on the attractiveness or unattractiveness of the object. *Attachment* comes from thirst. Through this thirst, one wants to be free from suffering and one wants to meet with and stay close to happiness. *Grasping* is the strong intention to take rebirth. There are four types of grasping: desirous grasping, grasping for views, grasping for ethics and modes of conduct and grasping for a self. Because one is born within cyclic existence there is *existence*. Because one has taken birth in the three realms, one acquires the impressions from karma and afflictive emotions. Through this, one continues to take rebirth. Birth comes about from the arising of the aggregates. *Birth* is the arising of the previously non-existent body aggregate of any species, such as that of a god or human. *Aging* comes from the maturing of the aggregates. Just as fruit decays after it ripens, aging is the development of grey hair and wrinkles. *Death* is caused by decomposition. Death comes about after one's warmth and consciousness disappear upon the exhaustion of one's lifespan. *Mourning* is the suffering that arises when one becomes afraid that one will become separated from one's friends, relatives and wealth. *Lamentation* is the speaking about one's mourning and the accompanying feeling of depression. *Suffering* is the unhappiness that comes from the decline of the body. Unhappiness is the unhappiness that comes from the decline of the mind. *Agitation* is the anxiety which comes from remembering one's previous mistakes.

D. THE CESSATION OF THE 12 LINKS OF INTERNAL DEPENDENT ARISING

[These only lead to the cessation of suffering.]

1) the cessation of ignorance (མ་རིག་པ་འགགས་པ།)

2) the cessation of action (འདུ་བྱེད་འགགས་པ།)

3) the cessation of consciousness (རྣམ་པར་ཤེས་པ་འགགས་པ།)

4) the cessation of name and form (མིང་དང་གཟུགས་འགགས་པ།)

5) the cessation of the six sources (སྐྱེ་མཆེད་དྲུག་འགགས་པ།)

6) the cessation of contact (རེག་པ་འགགས་པ།)

7) the cessation of feeling (ཚོར་བ་འགགས་པ།)

8) the cessation of attachment (སྲེད་པ་འགགས་པ།)

9) the cessation of grasping (ལེན་པ་འགགས་པ།)

10) the cessation of existence (སྲིད་པ་འགགས་པ།)

11) the cessation of birth (སྐྱེ་བ་འགགས་པ།)

12) the cessation of aging, death, mourning, lamentation , suffering, unhappiness and agitation (རྒ་ཤི་དང་། སྨུ་ངན་དང་། སྨྲེ་ སྔགས་འདོན་པ་དང་། སྡུག་བསྔལ་བ་དང་། ཡིད་མི་བདེ་བ་དང་། འཁྲུགས་པ་རྣམས་ འགགས།)

E. THE SIX CAUSES OF INTERNAL DEPENDENT ARISING (རྒྱུ།)

1) earth (ས།)

2) water (ཆུ།)

3) fire (མེ།)

4) air (རླུང་།)

5) space (ནམ་མཁའ།)

6) consciousness (རྣམ་པར་ཤེས་པ།)

F. THE FIVE CHARACTERISTICS ONE VIEWS WITHIN DEPENDENT ARISING (རྟེན་པ་ལྟར་ལྟ་བ།)

1) impermanence (རྟག་པར་མ་ཡིན་པ།)

2) absence of nihilistic qualities (ཆད་པར་མ་ཡིན་པ།)

3) non-production of inherently existent phenomena
(འཕོ་བ་མ་ཡིན་པ།)

4) large results which stem from small causes
(རྒྱུ་ཆུང་དུ་ལས་འབྲས་བུ་ཆེན་པོ།)

5) the mental continuum in which these results are manifested
(དེ་དང་འདྲ་བའི་རྒྱུ།)

6. THE SIX CAUSES (རྒྱུ།)

a. acting cause (བྱེད་པའི་རྒྱུ།)

b. innately-born cause (ལྷན་ཅིག་འབྱུང་བའི་རྒྱུ།)

c. equal-state cause (སྐལ་བ་མཉམ་པའི་རྒྱུ།)

d. concomitant cause (མཚུངས་པར་ལྟན་པའི་རྒྱུ།)

e. omnipresent cause (ཀུན་དུ་འགྲོ་བའི་རྒྱུ།)

f. ripening cause (རྣམ་པར་སྨིན་པའི་རྒྱུ།)

The *acting causes* are those that do not block the arising of a phenomenon. That which does not block the growth of a sprout is an acting cause by virtue of its not blocking the growth. The *innately-born* causes are like earth, water, fire or air, which all exist in any one particle. In order for one to arise, all four elements must act as the cause. Thus each element depends on each other element. The way in which they arise simultaneously is similar to the way in which one person cannot go alone to a frightening place. After several people gather together, they accompany each other and are delivered from the fear. The *equal-state cause* refers to the arising of mental factors that are in accordance with the state of mind. Thus if one has a virtuous state of mind, virtuous mental factors will arise, while non-virtuous mental factors arise from non-virtuous states of mind. The *concomitant cause* also refers to the relationship between the mind and mental factors. Neither the mind nor mental factors alone can penetrate and analyze an object. The mind and the many mental factors act as reciprocal causes. Because they accompany each other, they occur simultaneously. Whereas in the previous example, there were several companions who merely accompanied one to the frightening place, in this situation, these companions will not allow one to stay in one place. They push and shove one to a certain area. In this way, similar to the mental factors and the mind, these helpers lead one to a certain place. The *omnipresent cause* refers to births in the desire realm, the four concentrations of the form realm and the four formless absorptions of the formless realm, which cause the future rebirth in a body with afflictive emotions. The *ripening cause* refers to the causes of virtuous actions which result in higher rebirth and non-virtuous actions which result in lower rebirth.

7. THE FOUR CONDITIONS (རྐྱེན།)

1) objective conditions (དམིགས་རྐྱེན།)

2) fundamental conditions (བདག་པོའི་རྐྱེན།)

3) immediate condition (དེ་མ་ཐག་རྐྱེན།)

4) causal condition (རྒྱུ་རྐྱེན།)

The six external objects such as form and sound are the *objective conditions* of consciousness. Because the five sense powers such as the eye sense power are responsibl for the generation of consciousness, they are called *fundamental conditions*. Because the mental consciousness follows immediately after the cessation of the mental sense power, it is called the *immediate condition*. The mind as the basis-of-all acts as a cause and a condition and is thus called a *causal condition*.

8. THE FIVE TYPES OF RESULTS (འབྲས་བུ།)

a. ripened results (རྣམ་པར་སྨིན་པའི་འབྲས་བུ།)

b. results that accord with the cause (རྒྱུ་མཐུན་གྱི་འབྲས་བུ།)

c. cessational results (བྲལ་བའི་འབྲས་བུ།)

d. results caused by persons (སྐྱེ་བུའི་བྱེད་པའི་འབྲས་བུ།)

e. environmental results (བདག་པོའི་འབྲས་བུ།)

Ripened results refers to effects such as generosity leading to wealth, stealing leading to poverty, and killing or hurting leading to a short life or many illnesses. *Results that accord with the cause* refers to the desire to do virtuous activities in this life if one did virtuous activities in past lives, or the desire to do negative actions in this life if one performed negativities in past lives. *Cessational results* is the abandonment of afflictive emotions after one meditates on the Arya path. *Results caused by persons* include the accrual of many barley sprouts when one does farming, the accrual of many goods by doing business, or the accrual of many livestock by animal husbandry. *Environmental results* refers to the quality of the location of one's birth. If one performed negativities in previous lives, then one is born in a bad location. If one performed virtuous activities, then one is born in a good location.

9. THE TWO TRUTHS (བདེན་པ།)

A. CONVENTIONAL TRUTH (ཀུན་རྫོབ་ཀྱི་བདེན་པ།)

1) correct conventional truth (ཡང་དག་པའི་ཀུན་རྫོབ།)

2) incorrect conventional truth (ཡང་དག་མ་ཡིན་པའི་ཀུན་རྫོབ།)

B. ULTIMATE TRUTH (དོན་དམ་པའི་བདེན་པ།)

10. THE THREE NATURES (མཚན་ཉིད།)

a. imputed phenomena (ཀུན་བཏགས།)

b. dependent phenomena (གཞན་དབང་།)

c. thoroughly established phenomena (ཡོངས་གྲུབ།)

The mistaken imputation of inherent existence onto the six objects of consciousness such as form, the six sense powers, phenomena and individuals is what is known as *imputed phenomena*. The mode in which the mind as the basis-of-all and the neighboring consciousnesses exist is a string of moments consisting of causes and results. This mode of existence is called *dependent phenomena*. The non-conceptual wisdom which understands the emptiness of dharma spheres is called *thoroughly established phenomena*.

11. THE FIVE PHENOMENA (ཆོས་ལྔ།)

a. name (མིང་།)

b. reasoning (རྒྱུ་མཚན།)

c. conceptualization (རྣམ་པར་རྟོག་པ།)

d. suchness (དེ་བཞིན་ཉིད།)

e. perfect wisdom (ཡང་དག་པའི་ཡེ་ཤེས།)

All phenomena are included in the conglomeration of these five phenomena. A *name*, or categorization, in and of itself is not an object of consciousness. One cannot explain why arbitrary sounds are attached to certain objects. Yet in order to illustrate symbolically the significance of the object of examination, one attaches a name to it. *Reason* refers to the reciprocal relation between the mind as the basis-of-all which is the cause, and the other seven consciousnesses, which are the result. (This term can be rendered into English as either 'reason' or 'suitability'. There is substantiation for both. Yet 'reason' is in accord with the accompanying commentary. Furthermore, some translate the terms as 'awareness' stemming from a different Tibetan spelling i.e. 'rig pa'.) Through the eight consciousnesses, one conceptualizes the characteristics of phenomena such as the solidity of earth or the fluidity of water, their natures, their impermanence or their suffering. Thus one speaks of *conceptualization*. All phenomena are not inherently produced. Rather they are empty of inherent existence, and this is called *suchness*. Unmistaken, thoroughly established pure wisdom is called *perfect wisdom*.

12. THE TWO SELFLESSNESSES (བདག་མེད་པ།)

a. the selflessness of phenomena (ཆོས་ལ་བདག་མེད་པ།)

b. the selflessness of beings (གང་ཟག་ལ་བདག་མེད་པ།)

13. THE THREE VEHICLES (ཐེག་པ།)

a. Hearer (ཉན་ཐོས་ཀྱི་ཐེག་པ།)

b. Solitary Realizer (རང་སངས་རྒྱས་ཀྱི་ཐེག་པ།)

c. Mahayana (ཐེག་པ་ཆེན་པོ།)

Through reliance on the spiritual guide, one develops an understanding of the four truths and of the four individual characteristics of each. Through this, one perceives the selflessness of individuals and abandons all obscurations of passions. This state is called the state of a *Hearer*. Without relying on a teacher, one perceives the characteristics of dependent arising and its cessation. Then one perceives the selflessness of individuals and abandons all obscurations of passions. This state is called the state of *Solitary Realizer*. One gradually achieves the six perfections and the 10 Bodhisattva grounds and perceives the selflessness of phenomena and of individuals. Then one abandons both obscurations of passion and wisdom. This state is called the true attainment of the *Mahayana*.

14. THE THREE JEWELS (དཀོན་མཆོག)

A. Buddha (སངས་རྒྱས་དཀོན་མཆོག)

B. Dharma (ཆོས་དཀོན་མཆོག)

C. Sangha (དགེ་འདུན་དཀོན་མཆོག)

15. THE 37 LIMBS OF ENLIGHTENMENT (བྱང་ཆུབ་ཀྱི་ཕྱོགས།)

The 37 limbs of enlightenment are the ways of contemplating the stages and antidotes leading to enlightenment. Enlightenment is the achievement of the wisdom of exhaustive , complete perception of emptiness and the lack of inherent production, which is in the mental continuums of the Hearers, Solitary Realizers and Bodhisattvas. The stages are the 10 grounds of a Bodhisattva. The antidotes are the abandonment and aversion to those qualities (such as miserliness) which are not compatible with the 10 grounds. This is similar to an enemy and his opponent.

A. THE FOUR CLOSE CONTEMPLATIONS (དྲན་པ་ཉེ་བར་བཞག་པ།)

1) close contemplation of the body (ལུས་དྲན་པ་ཉེ་བར་བཞག་པ།)

2) close contemplation of feelings (ཚོར་བ་དྲན་པ་ཉེ་བར་བཞག་པ།)

3) close contemplation of the mind (སེམས་དྲན་པ་ཉེ་བར་བཞག་པ།)

4) close contemplation of phenomena (ཆོས་དྲན་པ་ཉེ་བར་བཞག་པ།)

By single-pointed contemplation of the object of examination through correct wisdom, one practices calm abiding. This is close contemplation. *Close contemplation of the body* is of three types: the internal body, which is one's own body; the external body, which consists of forms without consciousness such as trees; and the internal body of those in the external world, which includes the bodies of sentient beings and inanimate objects that are outside of oneself. The specific characteristics of the internal body are birth and change, which result in disintegration and destruction. Their general characteristics are impermanence and suffering. One must identify these characteristics and the nature of the impurities such as pus, lymph and phlegm, which fill the body from head to toe. The internal body of those in the external world is similar to one's own internal body. The specific characteristic of the external body is that it is a combination of minute particles. Its general characteristics are the same as the internal body. After one has ascertained these characteristics through wisdom, one contemplates them single-pointedly. The *close contemplation of feelings* has three correlated aspects. The three types of feelings which arise when one focuses on the internal body are called the internal feelings. Those that arise when one focuses on the external body are called external feelings. Those that arise upon focusing on the internal body of those in the external world are called the internal-external feelings. As for the three types of feelings that arise, contentment of body and mind is called happiness. Unhappiness of body and mind is called suffering. When neither of these feelings are present, this state is neutrality. The general characteristics of these feelings are the same as those of the internal body. The specific nature of these is suffering. The feeling of suffering is the suffering of suffering. The feeling of happiness is the suffering of change. The feeling of neutrality is the suffering of all-pervasive conditioning. One identifies these characteristics and contemplates them single-pointedly. The *close contemplation of the mind* involves an examination of 20 factors which occur in pairs: desire and a mind free from desire, hatred and freedom from hatred, ignorance and freedom from ignorance, gathering within of the mind and wandering to external objects, depression and upliftment, excitement and lack of excitement, pacification and lack of pacification, meditative absorption and lack of meditative absorption, meditation on the path and liberation from meditation on the path, and lack of liberation through meditation on the path. The first six of these factors are considered trainings because they are to be practiced. The remaining factors are considered abidings because they are states of engagement in stabilization. When these factors arise in connection with the internal body, they are considered to be the internal mind. When they arise in connection with the external body, they are considered to be the external mind. When they arise in connection with the internal body of those in the external world, they are considered to be the internal-external mind. One contemplates single-pointedly the impermanence, suffering, emptiness and selflessness of all these phenomena. The *close contemplation of phenomena* is the contemplation of the afflictive emotions and purification. The above-mentioned 20 factors and the secondary afflictive emotions are all afflictive emotions. Purification refers to the antidote to the afflictive emotions, which is their abandonment. It consists of an understanding of the impure nature of the body, an understanding of love and an understanding of dependent arising. One must realize and meditate on these phenomena, their emptiness of inherent existence and their selflessness.

B. THE FOUR PERFECT ABANDONMENTS (ཡང་དག་པར་སྤོང་བ།)

1) the generation of the aspiration to not generate non-virtues that have not yet been produced (སྡིག་པ་མི་དགེ་བའི་ཆོས་མ་སྐྱེ་བ་རྣམས་ མི་བསྐྱེད་པར་བྱ་བའི་ཕྱིར་འདུན་པ་བསྐྱེད་པ།)

2) the generation of the aspiration to abandon non-virtues that have been produced (སྡིག་པ་མི་དགེ་བའི་ཆོས་སྐྱེས་པ་རྣམས་སྤོང་བའི་ཕྱིར་འདུན་ པ་བསྐྱེད་པ།)

3) the generation of the aspiration to generate virtues that have not yet been produced (དགེ་བའི་ཆོས་མ་སྐྱེ་བ་རྣམས་བསྐྱེད་པའི་ཕྱིར་འདུན་པ་ བསྐྱེད་པ།)

4) the generation of the aspiration to sustain without decline and to perfect virtues that have been produced (དགེ་བའི་ཆོས་སྐྱེས་པ་ རྣམས་གནས་པར་བྱ་བ་དང་། ཕྱིར་ཞིང་འབྱུང་བ་དང་། རྣམས་པར་མི་འགྱུར་བ་ དང་། ཡོངས་སུ་རྫོགས་པར་བྱ་བའི་ཕྱིར་འདུན་པ་བསྐྱེད་པ།)

The four perfect abandonments are the four types of enthusiastic actions that accompany the realizations one obtains when one engages in close contemplation of phenomena. These realizations are the awareness that the afflictive emotions are non conducive with a pure practice, and that purification is the antidote to them, which requires their abandonment. Among the 10 non-virtues, three are actions of the body, four are actions of speech and three are actions of mind. The causes of these actions arising , such as desire and anger, ripen to become great suffering. Therefore their generation is called negativity. These non-virtues are not consistent with virtuous activity, and they lower one's position among the Aryas. By focusing on these non-virtues as the object, one accumulates impressions on one's mental continuum through these actions. Therefore, this process is called generation. If the impressions are not accumulated, then there is no generation. Aspiration is the train of thought that concentrates on not generating these negativities in the present, not allowing them to arise in the future, and causing the definite cessation of those generated in the past. Thus one thoroughly avoids and abandons them. Virtues are the opposite of the non-virtues stated above. They consist of the 10 virtues which are non-attachment, non-hatred and so forth. The term abandonment refers to the perfect abandonment of everything that is not compatible with the Dharma through virtuous actions. Sustaining is the thought that will truly accomplish the cultivation within one's mental continuum of whatever virtue has not been previously cultivated. Furthermore, that small virtue which is already present should increase without decline.

C. THE FOUR LEGS OF MIRACLES (རྫུ་འཕྲུལ་གྱི་རྐང་པ།)

1) the concentration on aspiration with the application of the eight antidotes (འདུན་པའི་ཏིང་ངེ་འཛིན་སྐྱོང་བའི་འདུ་བྱེད་དང་ལྡན་པའི་རྫུ་འཕྲུལ་གྱི་རྐང་པ།)

2) the concentration of mind with the application of the eight antidotes (སེམས་ཀྱི་ཏིང་ངེ་འཛིན་སྐྱོང་བའི་འདུ་བྱེད་དང་ལྡན་པའི་རྫུ་འཕྲུལ་གྱི་རྐང་པ།)

3) the concentration on perseverance with the application of the eight antidotes (བརྩོན་འགྲུས་ཀྱི་ཏིང་ངེ་འཛིན་སྐྱོང་བའི་འདུ་བྱེད་དང་ལྡན་པའི་རྫུ་འཕྲུལ་གྱི་རྐང་པ།)

4) the concentration on analysis with the application of the eight antidotes (དཔྱོད་པའི་ཏིང་ངེ་འཛིན་སྐྱོང་བའི་འདུ་བྱེད་དང་ལྡན་པའི་རྫུ་འཕྲུལ་གྱི་རྐང་པ།)

'Miracle' refers to the five exceptional powers. The causes of the four legs are the four common practices of concentration. ['Common' here means that it is common to both Hinayana and Mahayana practice.] Through the power of fondness and aspiration, one's concentration reaches fruition. Thus by way of constant concentration, one achieves single-pointedness. This concentration is called the concentration on aspiration. It is the nature of this concentration to want to attain the results which are the qualities of higher rebirth and emancipation. There are five obscurations that are not conducive to concentration. These are laziness, losing the meditative support, lethargy or excitement, not applying the antidotes and distraction through too much gathering within. The first four antidotes, which are aspiration, effort, faith and suppleness, are the antidotes to laziness. The antidote to losing the meditative support is mindfulness. Introspection is the antidote to lethargy or excitement. Watchfulness is the antidote to not applying the antidotes, and equanimity is the antidote to distraction through too much gathering within. The concentration of mind is the attainment of single-pointedness through the force of the effect of the long-term practice of stabilization meditation in previous lives.

The concentration on perseverance is the single- pointedness one achieves through unceasing effort in abandoning non-virtuous activities and cultivating virtuous activities. The concentration on analysis is the single-pointedness that is attained by analysis, without doubt, that ascertains the important characteristics of phenomena such as impermanence and emptiness through the teachings and wisdom one receives from one's spiritual guide.

D. The Five Powers (དབང་པོ།)

1) the power of faith (དད་པའི་དབང་པོ།)

2) the power of effort (བརྩོན་འགྲུས་ཀྱི་དབང་པོ།)

3) the power of mindfulness (དྲན་པའི་དབང་པོ།)

4) the power of concentration (ཏིང་ངེ་འཛིན་གྱི་དབང་པོ།)

5) the power of wisdom (ཤེས་རབ་ཀྱི་དབང་པོ།)

'Power' refers to the empowerment given by these factors to obtain the elements conducive to enlightenment and to cultivate the roots of virtue. *Faith* is the combination of conviction, faith and aspiration. If one has faith, one can be delivered from cyclic existence. With this thought, one develops *effort*. Effort empowers one to accomplish the three trainings. The *power of mindfulness* empowers one to have superior ethical conduct. The *power of concentration* empowers one to have superior thought. The *power of wisdom* empowers one to have superior wisdom. Furthermore , each power empowers the proceeding power. For example, faith empowers effort.

E. The Five Forces (སྟོབས།)

1) the force of faith (དད་པའི་སྟོབས།)

2) the force of effort (བརྩོན་འགྲུས་ཀྱི་སྟོབས།)

3) the force of mindfulness (དྲན་པའི་སྟོབས།)

4) the force of concentration (ཏིང་ངེ་འཛིན་གྱི་སྟོབས།)

5) the force of wisdom (ཤེས་རབ་ཀྱི་སྟོབས།)

The forces prevent wavering towards factors that are not conducive to enlightenment, such as non-faith, laziness, losing the meditative support, distraction, and lack of introspection. The difference between the powers and the forces can be understood in terms of the four conducive factors which separate the elements not conducive to enlightenment from the conducive elements. These four factors are the conceptual understanding of emptiness, the enhancement of this, the direct perception of emptiness as conceived through a conceptual understanding, and the moment of thought that immediately precedes the direct perception of emptiness. At the time that one understands inferentially that the name and identity attached to an object are illusory, this is the conceptual understanding of emptiness. When one understands inferentially that the actual object that is referred to by this name is illusory, this is the enhancement of this understanding. The five powers are achieved during these two periods. At that time when one understands that the name and identity attached to an object are empty of inherent existence, then this is considered to be direct perception of emptiness as conceived of through a conceptual understanding. When one understands that the actual object that is referred to by this name is empty of inherent existence then this is the moment of thought that immediately precedes the direct perception of emptiness. One who has attained the path of seeing has obtained both the five powers and the five forces.

F. THE SEVEN AUXILIARIES TO ENLIGHTENMENT

(བྱང་ཆུབ་ཡན་ལག་)

1) the mindfulness auxiliary of perfect enlightenment (དྲན་པ་ཡང་དག་བྱང་ཆུབ་ཀྱི་ཡན་ལག་)

2) the wisdom auxiliary of perfect enlightenment (ཆོས་རྣམ་པར་འབྱེད་པ་ཡང་དག་བྱང་ཆུབ་ཀྱི་ཡན་ལག་)

3) the effort auxiliary of perfect enlightenment (རྩོན་འགྲུས་ཡང་དག་བྱང་ཆུབ་ཀྱི་ཡན་ལག་)

4) the joy auxiliary of perfect enlightenment (དགའ་བ་ཡང་དག་བྱང་ཆུབ་ཀྱི་ཡན་ལག་)

5) the suppleness auxiliary of perfect enlightenment (ཤིན་ཏུ་སྦྱངས་པ་ཡང་དག་བྱང་ཆུབ་ཀྱི་ཡན་ལག་)

6) the concentration auxiliary of perfect enlightenment (ཏིང་ངེ་འཛིན་ཡང་དག་བྱང་ཆུབ་ཀྱི་ཡན་ལག་)

7) the equanimity auxiliary of perfect enlightenment (བྱང་ཆུབ་ཡན་ ་

དག་བྱང་ཆུབ་ཀྱི་ཡན་ལག)

The term enlightenment in the phrase 'the seven auxiliaries to enlightenment' refers to the understanding of the emptiness of all phenomena and the wisdom that sees the impermanence of all appearances. The principal auxiliary is the wisdom auxiliary. The others accompany this one. Pure *mindfulness* is the auxiliary of abiding where wisdom abides. If one has mindfulness, then through the arising and cultivation of wisdom, abides in this mindfulness. *Wisdom* is the auxiliary of nature because it is the perception of actual characteristics of phenomena. *Effort* is the auxiliary of renunciation because it leads to the renunciation of an ordinary individual's circumstance, and thus one goes beyond this state. *Joy* is the auxiliary of fortune because the joy one receives at attaining the first Bodhisattva ground gives the body and mind such fortuitous benefits and contentment. *Suppleness*, concentration, and equanimity are all auxiliaries without afflictive emotions. Suppleness is the basis of this lack of afflictive emotions. This lack of afflictive emotions abides in *concentration*. *Equanimity* is the actual nature of this state of being without afflictive emotions. This relationship between the auxiliaries and the lack of afflictive emotions exists because attachment, desire and so forth cannot arise if one holds one's body and mind appropriately, that is, with suppleness. Through single-pointedness, or concentration, one abandons all the objects of abandonment of the path of seeing. After one abandons these objects, then from that point on, afflictive emotions such as desire do not arise. This comes about because the mental continuum, which is the nature of purity, enters into a state of equanimity.

G. THE EIGHTFOLD NOBLE PATH (འཕགས་པའི་ལམ་ཡན་ལག)

1) right view (ཡང་དག་པའི་ལྟ་བ)

2) right thought (ཡང་དག་པའི་རྟོག་པ)

3) right speech (ཡང་དག་པའི་ངག)

4) right action (ཡང་དག་པའི་ལས་ཀྱི་མཐའ)

5) right livelihood (ཡང་དག་པའི་འཚོ་བ)

6) right effort (ཡང་དག་པའི་རྩོལ་བ)

7) right mindfulness (ཡང་དག་པའི་དྲན་པ།)

8) right concentration (ཡང་དག་པའི་ཏིང་ངེ་འཛིན།)

The term 'noble' ('phags pa, Arya) in 'eightfold noble path' refers to a person who has completely abandoned all the afflictive emotions (such as attachment) which are the objects of abandonment of the path of seeing and meditation. These eight paths are the cause of the attainment of the rank of an Arya. Although these paths are called the noble paths, they are actually the paths of the specific types of wisdom of a Superior, or Arya. *Right view* is the pure worldly wisdom without discursive thought that is a characteristic of a person on the second Bodhisattva ground and higher. It is followed by a post-meditative state. Through non-discursive wisdom, which has spheres of phenomena as its object, one sees things as they are. One then proceeds to analyze what is seen, and this is called the limb of perfect analysis. *Right thought* is the unerring examination of the specific and general characteristics of phenomena. One explains to others through pure speech the phenomena in exactly the way one has realized them. Through these teachings, one's realizations and speech become the limb that makes others understand. *Right speech* consists of the unerring explanations given as answers to those who question or doubt the teachings. This is pure wisdom, and it is the limb which causes others to believe. *Right action* means that one has completely abandoned all non-virtuous conduct, and it is the limb which causes others to believe. *Right livelihood* is the lack of desire for material wealth. After the number of one's possessions has been reduced, one only looks for the possessions that one needs to perform virtuous activities. Thus one's income becomes moderate and one minimizes one's possessions. This is the limb which causes others to believe. Because right speech, right action, and right livelihood are faultless, they are the limb which causes others to believe. *Right effort* is the abandonment of even the hidden afflictive emotions such as desire, which are the objects of abandonments of the meditation. *Right mindfulness* is the abandonment of the secondary afflictive emotions. If lethargy or excitement arise, then one uses single-pointedness to correct the situation. In this way, even the secondary afflictive emotions are abandoned. *Right concentration* is the abandonment of all obscurations to the six extraordinary wisdoms. Because they result in the extraordinary wisdoms, right effort, mindfulness and concentration are called the antidotes to factors not conducive to enlightenment.

16. THE FIVE PATHS (ལམ།)

A. PATH OF ACCUMULATION (ཚོགས་ཀྱི་ལམ།)

1) the ethical conduct of one who has just entered the path (སོ་སོ་སྐྱེ་ བོའི་ཚུལ་ཁྲིམས།)

2) the restraint of the senses [from objects of attachment] (དབང་པོའི་སྒོ་ བསྡམས་པ།)

3) the restriction of one's food intake (ཟས་ཀྱི་ཚོད་ཤེས་པ།)

4) the refraining from sleep in the evening and at dawn and the enthusiastic practice of yoga during those periods (ནམ་ཀྱི་ཆ་ སྟོད་ཆ་སྨད་ལ་མི་ཉལ་བར་རྣལ་འབྱོར་ལ་བརྩོན་པ།)

5) the thorough enjoyment of abiding in introspection (ཤེས་བཞིན་དུ་ གནས་པ་ལ་མངོན་པར་དགའ་བ།)

B. PATH OF PREPARATION (སྦྱོར་ལམ།)

1) the concentration on the conceptual understanding of emptiness (སྟོང་བ་ཐོབ་པའི་ཏིང་ངེ་འཛིན།)

2) the enhancement of this concentration (སྟོང་བ་མཆེད་པའི་ཏིང་ངེ་འཛིན།)

3) the direct perception of emptiness as conceived of through a conceptual understanding (དེ་ཁོ་ནའི་དོན་ཚིག་གི་ཕྱོགས་གཅིག་ཏུ་ཞུགས་ པའི་ཏིང་ངེ་འཛིན།)

4) the moment of thought that immediately precedes the direct perception of emptiness (དེ་མ་ཐག་པ་སེམས་ཀྱི་ཏིང་ངེ་འཛིན།)

C. PATH OF SEEING (མཐོང་བའི་ལམ།)

This path consists of the first Bodhisattva ground.

D. PATH OF MEDITATION (བསྒོམ་པའི་ལམ།)

This path comprises the second to the 10th Bodhisattva grounds.

E. PATH OF PERFECTION (མཐར་ཕྱིན་པའི་ལམ།)

This is the Buddha ground.

The five routes by which one goes from the state of an ordinary individual to the state of an Arya are called the five paths. These paths can be joined with the 37 limbs of enlightenment. After one has generated the thought of enlightenment, one meditates on the four close contemplations, the four perfect abandonments, and the four legs of miracles. Thus one accumulates merit, and this is the path of accumulation. One meditates on the five powers and the five forces. Thus, by generating aspiration one abides on the level of practice. This is called the path of preparation. When one meditates on the seven auxiliaries to enlightenment, one attains the first Bodhisattva ground. This is called the path of seeing. When one meditates on the eight-fold noble path, one abides in each of the Bodhisattva grounds from the second to the 10th level. This is called the path of meditation. The path of perfection is the abiding on the level of omnipresent light by a Buddha, or a Hearer's accomplishment of the state of Foe Destroyer.

17. THE 10 PERFECTIONS (ཕ་རོལ་ཏུ་ཕྱིན་པ།)

a. the perfection of generosity (སྦྱིན་པའི་ཕ་རོལ་ཏུ་ཕྱིན་པ།)

b. the perfection of ethical discipline
(ཚུལ་ཁྲིམས་ཀྱི་ཕ་རོལ་ཏུ་ཕྱིན་པ།)

c. the perfection of patience (བཟོད་པའི་ཕ་རོལ་ཏུ་ཕྱིན་པ།)

d. the perfection of enthusiastic perseverance
(བརྩོན་འགྲུས་ཀྱི་ཕ་རོལ་ཏུ་ཕྱིན་པ།)

e. the perfection of meditative equipoise
(བསམ་གཏན་གྱི་ཕ་རོལ་ཏུ་ཕྱིན་པ།)

f. the perfection of wisdom (ཤེས་རབ་ཀྱི་ཕ་རོལ་ཏུ་ཕྱིན་པ།)

g. the perfection of means (ཐབས་ཀྱི་ཕ་རོལ་ཏུ་ཕྱིན་པ།)

h. the perfection of power (སྟོབས་ཀྱི་ཕ་རོལ་ཏུ་ཕྱིན་པ།)

i. the perfection of aspirational prayers

(སྨོན་ལམ་གྱི་ཕ་རོལ་ཏུ་ཕྱིན་པ།)

j. the perfection of primordial wisdom (ཡེ་ཤེས་ཀྱི་ཕ་རོལ་ཏུ་ཕྱིན་པ།)

These are called the 'perfections' (literally 'going to the other side') because one goes beyond the suffering of the three realms.

18. THE 10 BODHISATTVA GROUNDS (བྱང་ཆུབ་སེམས་པའི་ས།)

a. joyful (རབ་ཏུ་དགའ་བ།)

b. stainless (དྲི་མ་མེད་པ།)

c. illuminating (འོད་བྱེད་པ།)

d. radiant (འོད་འཕྲོ་བ།)

e. difficult to train (ཤིན་ཏུ་སྦྱང་དཀའ་བ།)

f. advancing (མངོན་དུ་གྱུར་བ།)

g. gone afar (རིང་དུ་སོང་བ།)

h. unwavering (མི་གཡོ་བ།)

i. excellent wisdom (ལེགས་པའི་བློ་གྲོས།)

j. cloud of Dharma (ཆོས་ཀྱི་སྤྲིན།)

k. the Buddha ground is the omnipresent light (ཀུན་ཏུ་འོད།)

The 10 grounds are the results of the 10 perfections, which act as their cause. They are connected in a consecutive manner. The first ground, *joyful*, is like a poor person who has found a valuable jewel such as he has never seen before. Similarly, a practitioner has never seen a Dharma sphere before as he actually sees it at that point. One is capable of fulfilling one's own and others' purposes in a supreme manner.

After one has accomplished the perfection of generosity, one generates limitless joy and thus this stage is called 'joyful'. The second ground, *stainless*, is free of the stains of enjoying the non-virtuous and compassionless activities of cyclic existence and of the Hinayana. Furthermore, having accomplished the perfection of ethical discipline, one does not even perform unethical activities in one's dreams. Thus this ground is called 'stainless'. After one accomplishes the perfection of patience, one seeks the teachings without regard for one's body or life. Thus one's own ignorance and the ignorance of others is cleared away, and the wisdom that is generated is called the ground of *'illuminating'*. The fourth ground is *radiant*. Through the accomplishment of the perfection of enthusiastic perseverance, one meditates on the practices of a Bodhisattva. This leads to the cultivation of a wisdom which, like a fire blazing in a forest, burns away afflictive emotions. Thus this ground is called 'radiant'. By accomplishing the perfection of meditative equipoise, one simultaneously trains in the cultivation of meditative stabilization that is unconceptualized wisdom and the unceasing fulfillment of others' purposes. Since this simultaneous training is very difficult, this stage is called *'difficult to train'*. Through the accomplishment of perfection of wisdom, one cognizes directly dependent arising and the unhindered nature of emptiness. Through this advancement to direct insight, this ground is called *advancing*. By the accomplishment of the perfection of means, one has reached the ground of *gone afar* because one becomes free of any indication of applying efforts. Having accomplished the perfection of power, one spontaneously realizes the lack of inherent existence of all phenomena. Since one has entirely overcome this view, this ground is called *unwavering*. Through the accomplishment of the perfection of aspirational prayers, one obtains the specific, perfect understandings of Dharma, meaning, definitive words, and confidence. Thus one becomes a great teacher, and so this ground is called *excellent wisdom*. Through the perfection of primordial wisdom, just as the rain from a huge cloud causes a barren land to grow crops, the huge cloud of this Bodhisattva's wisdom and compassion causes the barren minds of sentient beings to cultivate the crops of virtue. Thus this stage is called *cloud of Dharma*.

19. THE FOUR TYPES OF WISDOM OF THE BUDDHA

(སངས་རྒྱས་ཀྱི་ཡེ་ཤེས།)

a. mirror-like wisdom (མེ་ལོང་ལྟ་བུའི་ཡེ་ཤེས།)

b. wisdom of equality (མཉམ་པ་ཉིད་ཀྱི་ཡེ་ཤེས།)

c. wisdom of discrimination (སོ་སོར་རྟོག་པའི་ཡེ་ཤེས།)

d. wisdom of accomplishment (བྱ་བ་ནན་ཏན་གྱི་ཡེ་ཤེས།)

The four types of wisdom of a Buddha consist of the categorization of objects of consciousness that are understood to be pure by a Buddha. When an ordinary individual attains enlightenment, all eight consciousnesses are transformed. After the mind as the basis-of-all becomes purified of its stains, it is called *mirror-like wisdom*. When the afflicted consciousness becomes purified of its stains of the egoistic view, then it no longer distinguishes between self and other and thus is called the *wisdom of equality*. When the mental consciousness becomes purified of its stains such as attachment, it is called the *wisdom of discrimination*. When the five sense consciousnesses are purified of their stains of the conceptualization of phenomena as existing in isolation from each other, this is called the *wisdom of accomplishment*.

20. THE THREE BODIES OF BUDDHA (སངས་རྒྱས་ཀྱི་སྐུ་གསུམ།)

a. wisdom body (ཆོས་ཀྱི་སྐུ།)

b. complete enjoyment body (ལོངས་སྤྱོད་ཀྱི་སྐུ།)

c. manifestation body (སྤྲུལ་པའི་སྐུ།)

The wisdom which acts like a mirror of Dharma spheres is called the *wisdom body*. The body that abides in the palace in heaven where teachings are given to the Bodhisattvas on the 10th ground and is adorned with the major and minor marks is called the *complete enjoyment body*. The body presented to the world as the Buddha Shakyamuni is the *manifestation body*.

21. THE FOUR SPECIFIC PERFECT UNDERSTANDINGS OF THOSE WHO HAVE GONE BEYOND (དེ་བཞིན་གཤེགས་པའི་སོ་སོར་ཡང་དག་པར་རིག་པ།)

a. specific perfect understanding of dharmas (ཆོས་སོ་སོར་ཡང་དག་པར་རིག་པ།)

b. specific perfect understanding of meaning (དོན་སོ་སོར་ཡང་དག་པར་རིག་པ།)

c. specific perfect understanding of definitive words (ངེས་པའི་ཚིག་སོ་སོར་ཡང་དག་པར་རིག་པ།)

d. specific perfect understanding of confidence (སྐྱོབས་པ་སོ་སོར་ཡང་
དག་པ་རིག་པ།)

The 'specific perfect understandings' refer to the four categories of unerring understanding of certain characteristics of phenomena. The *specific perfect understanding of dharmas* is the knowledge that there are many different terms used for the same phenomenon, and there is no contradiction in the terms used. Thus one teaches about the 84,000 afflictive emotions in the minds of different sentient beings and various antidotes to these states. When teaching from the sutras, one teaches general meanings found within blocks of the sutras. One can give either the general or specific meaning. The *specific perfect understanding of meaning* refers to a Buddha's knowledge of the meanings of the words he uses when he teaches. Thus he understands the meaning of the general characteristics of impermanence, suffering, emptiness, and selflessness as well as the ultimate characteristics of no inherent production or cessation and no true subject-object duality. The *specific perfect understanding of definitive words* is the knowledge of the languages, communication patterns, and sounds of sentient beings. There are many different meanings to each word of a Buddha, so many different sentient beings understand him simultaneously. His words are without deception, distortion, redundancy, or senselessness. The people who like the Buddha's teachings are the people who are praised by the Aryas. The *specific perfect understanding of confidence* is what follows the other three specific perfect understandings. A Buddha listens to others' philosophies in which doubt about the Buddha's teachings is expressed. A Buddha, through his knowledge of the Dharma, clears away the doubts of those who listen to him. His words are meaningful, sweet like Brahma's words. slowly stated, without gaps, and without stuttering.

22. THE FOUR FEARLESSNESSES OF THOSE WHO HAVE GONE BEYOND (དེ་བཞིན་གཤེགས་པའི་མི་འཇིགས་པ།)

a. the fearlessness in connection with becoming enlightened through the thorough understanding of all phenomena (ཆོས་ཐམས་ཅད་
མངོན་པར་རྟོགས་པ་བྱང་ཆུབ་པ་ལ་མི་འཇིགས་པ།)

b. the fearlessness in connection with the wisdom that eliminates all contamination (ཟག་པ་ཐམས་ཅད་ཟད་པར་མཁྱེན་པ་ལ་མི་འཇིགས་པ།)

c. the fearlessness in connection with teaching others how to avoid hindrances (བར་དུ་གཅོད་པའི་ཆོས་རྣམས་གཞན་དུ་མི་འགྱུར་བར་ལུང་བསྟན་པ་ལ་མི་འཇིགས་པ།)

d. the fearlessness in connection with the accomplishment of the state of suchness, which is the path of renunciation, in order to achieve all excellences (ཕུན་སུམ་ཚོགས་པ་ཐམས་ཅད་འཐོབ་པར་འགྱུར་བ་ལ་ངེས་པར་འབྱུང་བའི་ལམ་དེ་བཞིན་ཉིད་དུ་གྱུར་པ་ལ་མི་འཇིགས་པ།)

The four fearlessnesses are the aspects of fearlessness that a Buddha has in terms of fulfilling his own excellent purposes as well as the excellent purposes of others. The *fearlessness in connection with becoming enlightened through the thorough understanding of all phenomena* and the *fearlessness in connection with the wisdom that eliminates all contamination* are fearlessnesses in terms of the Buddha's fulfilling his own excellent purpose. By understanding all produced and unproduced phenomena without exception, one obtains perfect enlightenment. Although there are those who argue that a Buddha does not have such understanding of all phenomena, the Buddha has no fear of their doubts. Thus this fearlessness is excellent wisdom. A Buddha has eliminated all his contaminations such as attachment, and he is aware of how others can exterminate all their contaminations. Although others argue that he has not eliminated all contaminations or that he does not know how others can exterminate their contaminations, he has no fear of their doubts. This fearlessness is called excellent abandonment. The *fearlessness in connection with teaching others how to avoid hindrances* and the *fearlessness in connection with the accomplishment of the state of suchness, which is the path of renunciation in order to achieve all excellences*, are fearlessnesses in terms of fulfilling others' purposes through teachings. A Buddha is not afraid to teach others how to apply the antidotes to them. Thus he teaches that sensory stimuli are obstructions to the state of emancipation, which goes beyond the nature of suffering. Although some argue that these stimuli are not obstructions, a Buddha has no fear of these doubts and does not waver. This fearlessness is called the teaching of the abandonment of discordant factors. All excellences are the excellences of wisdom and abandonment. In order to achieve them, one follows the path of renunciation, which is the path of an Arya. It is just as the Buddha instructed. Although others argue that one does not achieve these excellences through this path, a Buddha is not afraid of their doubt. This fearlessness is the teaching of the correct path, which is the antidote.

23. THE SIX EXTRAORDINARY KNOWLEDGES OF THOSE WHO HAVE GONE BEYOND (དེ་བཞིན་གཤེགས་པའི་མངོན་པར་ཤེས་པ།)

a. the divine eye (ལྷའི་མིག་)

b. the divine ear (ལྷའི་རྣ་བ།)

c. knowledge of others' thoughts (སེམས་ཀྱི་རྣམ་གྲངས་ཤེས་པ།)

d. knowledge of miracles (ལུས་ཀྱི་རྫུ་འཕྲུལ་ཤེས་པ།)

e. knowledge of recollecting past lives (སྔོན་གྱི་གནས་རྗེས་སུ་དྲན་པ།)

f. knowledge of the extinction of contamination (ཟག་པ་ཟད་པ་ཤེས་པ།)

Extraordinary knowledge is the realization or knowledge that perceives invisible phenomena from other places and times as if they are right in the immediate area. The *divine eye* sees forms regardless of their distance, and it sees where beings take rebirth after they die. The *divine ear* hears and understands various sounds, speeches, and other communicative noises. The *knowledge of others' thoughts* allows one to understand the conscious and unconscious thoughts of sentient beings. The *knowledge of miracles* allows one to resist being burnt, to fly, to control one's mass, to control one's quality, to walk on water, and to go through earth. The *knowledge recollecting past lives* allows one to remember one's string of rebirths and the events in these past lives. The *knowledge of the extinction of contamination* is the knowledge which understands which afflictions have to be abandoned during the path of seeing and the path of meditation as well as their order. One attains the wisdom which extinguishes and does not generate afflictive emotions.

24. THE 10 POWERS OF THOSE WHO HAVE GONE BEYOND (དེ་བཞིན་གཤེགས་པའི་སྟོབས།)

a. the power of knowing right from wrong (གནས་དང་གནས་མ་ཡིན་པ་མཁྱེན་པའི་སྟོབས།)

b. the power of knowing consequences of actions (ལས་ཀྱི་རྣམ་པར་སྨིན་པ་མཁྱེན་པའི་སྟོབས།)

c. the power of knowing various mental inclinations (མོས་པ་སྣ་ཚོགས་མཁྱེན་པའི་སྟོབས།)

d. the power of knowing various mental faculties (ཁམས་སྣ་ཚོགས་མཁྱེན་པའི་སྟོབས།)

e. the power of knowing various degrees of intelligence (དབང་པོ་མཆོག་དང་མཆོག་མ་ཡིན་པ་མཁྱེན་པའི་སྟོབས།)

f. the power of knowing the paths of all goals (ཐམས་ཅད་དུ་འགྲོ་བའི་ལམ་མཁྱེན་པའི་སྟོབས།)

g. the power of knowing concentration, emancipation, stabilization, meditative absorption, the ever-afflicted, and purified phenomena (བསམ་གཏན་དང་། རྣམ་པར་ཐར་པ་དང་། ཏིང་ངེ་འཛིན་དང་། སྙོམས་པར་འཇུག་པ་དང་། ཀུན་ནས་ཉོན་མོངས་པ་དང་། རྣམ་པར་བྱང་བ་དང་ལྡན་པ་ཐམས་ཅད་མཁྱེན་པའི་སྟོབས།)

h. the power of knowing past lives (སྔོན་གྱི་གནས་རྗེས་སུ་དྲན་པ་མཁྱེན་པའི་སྟོབས།)

i. the power of knowing deaths and births (འཆི་འཕོ་བ་དང་སྐྱེ་བ་མཁྱེན་པའི་སྟོབས།)

j. the power of knowing the exhaustion of contaminations (ཟག་པ་ཐམས་ཅད་ཟད་པར་མཁྱེན་པའི་སྟོབས།)

The 10 powers are the specific powers of the wisdom of a Buddha. The *power of knowing right from wrong* means a Buddha understands causes and non-causes. Karma and afflictive emotions are the cause of rebirth. An inherently existent self, a universal creator, and the god Indra are not the causes of rebirth. Furthermore, virtuous activities are the causes of rebirth in the upper realms, and are not the causes of rebirth in the lower realms. Non-virtuous activities are the causes of rebirth in the lower realms, and are not the causes of rebirth in the upper realms. The *power of knowing consequences of actions* means a Buddha has the power of understanding the accumulation of karma by individuals. If one engages in actions such as generosity and ethical conduct, one will achieve happy results such as higher rebirth and wealth. If one engages in actions such as killing, one will achieve the results of rebirth in the lower realms and suffering. The *power of knowing various mental inclinations* is the Buddha's knowledge of the various inclinations of individual sentient beings. Some sentient beings are inclined towards the great vehicle; some are inclined to the small vehicle. Some are inclined to the middle vehicle; some are inclined towards generosity; some are inclined to ethical conduct; and some are inclined to meditative equipoise. The *power of knowing various mental faculties* means that a Buddha is skilled at understanding why individuals are born with certain characteristics. One's fate might be to take rebirth as an individual without certainty as to which vehicle to enter, or one might not enter a vehicle at all. The Buddha understands the specific fates and previous impressions of individuals, which cause them to be reborn as beings of one of the six species of the desire realm. The *power of knowing various degrees of intelligence* is the Buddha's skill at knowing the level of an individual. Thus he understands that some individuals are of middle capacity, and that others are of dull faculties. The *power of knowing paths to all goals* is the Buddha's skill at understanding the cyclical pattern of rebirth as beings of the six species of the desire realm and the causes of such migration throughout all the three realms. He also is skilled at focusing on the paths which lead to higher rebirth and enlightenment. The *power of knowing concentration, emancipation , stabilization, meditative absorption, the ever-afflicted, and purified phenomena* refers to a Buddha's understanding that by entering into meditation on the four concentrations, the eight emancipations, stabilization on developing confidence and so forth, and the nine meditative absorptions existing in series, one removes all discordant obstacles, which are called the ever- afflicted. The development of the antidotes to these afflictive emotions is called purified phenomena.

A Buddha knows the ways in which faults arise and the ways in which one develops virtuous qualities when going through this process. The *power of knowing past lives* is the Buddha's skill at knowing the locations place of an individual's past rebirths, his names, his activities, his lifespans and his degrees of wealth. The power of knowing deaths and births is Buddha's skill at knowing the times and places of all the rebirths of sentient beings. The power of knowing the exhaustion of contaminations is the skill of knowing the exhaustion of contaminations, such as afflictive emotions, of sentient beings.

25. THE 10 CAPABILITIES [of Those Who Have Gone Beyond] (དབང་།)

a. the capability of controlling the length of one's own life (ཚེ་ལ་དབང་བ།)

b. the capability of giving provisions to sentient beings (ཡོ་བྱད་ལ་དབང་བ།)

c. the capability of controlling one's mind without hindrances (སེམས་ལ་དབང་བ།)

d. the capability of mitigating the consequences of others' negativities (ལས་ལ་དབང་བ།)

e. the capability of controlling one's rebirth (སྐྱེ་བ་ལ་དབང་བ།)

f. the capability of being resolute in one's aspiration (མོས་པ་ལ་དབང་ བ།)

g. the capability of having only pure prayers (སྨོན་ལམ་ལ་དབང་བ།)

h. the capability of performing miraculous deeds (རྫུ་འཕྲུལ་ལ་དབང་ བ།)

i. the capability of teaching the Dharma (ཆོས་ལ་དབང་བ།)

j. the capability of understanding all phenomena (ཡེ་ཤེས་ལ་དབང་བ།)

Sentient beings have no control over the 10 types of harm which they constantly experience. Bodhisattvas possess the 10 capabilities, which are the antidotes to these harms. The *capability of controlling the length of one's own life* means that one can remain for immeasurable aeons without birth or death. Thus one does not have the harm of death. The *capability of giving provisions to sentient beings* refers to a Bodhisattva's ability to fill all the space in the world with jewels through his miraculous powers. Thus he removes the harm of poverty. The *capability of controlling one's mind without hindrances* refers to the Bodhisattva's ability to enter into countless concentrations, such as developing confidence, through his wisdom. Thus he is free from afflictive emotions such as desire, lethargy or excitement. The *capability of mitigating the consequences of others' negativities* refers to a Bodhisattva's ability to cause an individual to be reborn in a higher rebirth even when the individual has performed non-virtuous activities. Thus he removes the harm of experiencing suffering for one's actions. Furthermore, although the Bodhisattva has performed virtuous activities, he has the power to cause himself to be reborn in the lower realms. The *capability of controlling one's rebirth* is a Bodhisattva's ability to manifest himself in any body in any location in cyclic existence in accordance with his wish. Even if he takes rebirth in the lower realms, the harm of the sufferings of the lower realms does not fall upon him. The *capability of being resolute in one's aspirations* means that a Bodhisattva thoroughly abandons any negative aspirations towards the Dharma. Also, if the Dharma were to be destroyed, he would fill the whole world with manifestations of Buddhas and spiritual friends who would give teachings to sentient beings. Thus the harm of the destruction of the Dharma does not arise. Because a Bodhisattva has accomplished the perception of exhaustion, this is also the capability to be resolute in one's aspirations. The *capability of having only pure prayers* refers to the prayers of a Bodhisattva who makes requests to eventually reach a pure land and complete enlightenment. He becomes empowered to fulfil his wishes just as he has prayed. Thus the harm of not accomplishing one's wishes does not arise. The *capability of performing miraculous deeds* refers to the ability of those in a pure land, whose pure manifestations can resist fire and can fly. These miraculous bodies are without obstructions, and can go anywhere in an instant. Thus the harm of not being capable of going anywhere for the sake of the Dharma does not exist. The *capability of teaching the Dharma* refers to a Bodhisattva's ability to understand all phenomena without exception, including mundane and supramundane phenomena, and produced and non-produced phenomena. Thus the harm of others' doubting one's understanding does not arise. The *capability of understanding all phenomena* means that a Bodhisattva has all good qualities such as the powers and fearlessnesses. Thus there is no harm from others' questioning one's abilities.

26. THE 18 UNSHARED ATTRIBUTES OF BUDDHAS

(སངས་རྒྱས་ཀྱི་ཆོས་མ་འདྲེས་པ།)

a. being without mistakes (དེ་བཞིན་གཤེགས་པ་ལ་འཁྲུལ་བ་མི་མངའ་བ།)

b. being without verbal mistakes (ཅ་ཅོ་མི་མངའ་བ།)

c. not decreasing in mindfulness (བརྗེལ་བ་མི་མངའ་བ།)

d. not ever not being in meditative equipoise (སེམས་མཉམ་པར་མ་བཞག་ པ་མེད་པ།)

e. non-discrimination of cyclic existence and nirvana as separate (ཐ་དད་པའི་འདུ་ཤེས་མེད་པ།)

f. not being uninterested (སོ་སོར་མ་བརྟགས་པའི་བཏང་སྙོམས་མེད་པ།)

g. aspiration without decline (འདུན་པ་ཉམས་པ་མེད་པ།)

h. effort without decline (བརྩོན་འགྲུས་ཉམས་པ་མེད་པ།)

i. mindfulness without decline (ཤེས་རབ་ཉམས་པ་མེད་པ།)

j. wisdom without decline (ཤེས་རབ་ཉམས་པ་མེད་པ།)

k. concentration without decline (ཏིང་ངེ་འཛིན་ཉམས་པ་མེད་པ།)

l. liberation without decline (རྣམ་པར་གྲོལ་བ་ཉམས་པ་མེད་པ།)

m. the governing of all bodily activities by wisdom (ལུས་ཀྱི་ལས་ཐམས་ ཅད་ཡེ་ཤེས་ཀྱི་སྔོན་དུ་འགྲོ་ཞིང་ཡེ་ཤེས་ཀྱི་རྗེས་སུ་འབྲང་བ།)

n. the governing of all verbal activities by wisdom (ངག་གི་ལས་ཐམས་ ཅད་ཡེ་ཤེས་ཀྱི་སྔོན་དུ་འགྲོ་ཞིང་ཡེ་ཤེས་ཀྱི་རྗེས་སུ་འབྲང་བ།)

o. the governing of all mental activities by wisdom (ཡིད་ཀྱི་ལས་ཐམས་ ཅད་ཡེ་ཤེས་ཀྱི་སྔོན་དུ་འགྲོ་ཞིང་ཡེ་ཤེས་ཀྱི་རྗེས་སུ་འབྲང་བ།)

p. the unobstructed wisdom which sees all objects from the past

(འདས་པའི་དུས་ལ་མ་ཆགས་མ་ཐོགས་པའི་ཡེ་ཤེས་མཐོང་བ་ལ་འཇུག་པ།)

q. the unobstructed wisdom which sees all objects from the future

(མ་འོང་པའི་དུས་ལ་མ་ཆགས་མ་ཐོགས་པའི་ཡེ་ཤེས་མཐོང་བ་ལ་འཇུག་པ།)

r. the unobstructed wisdom which sees all objects from the present

(ད་ལྟར་བ་ཞུགས་པའི་དུས་ལ་མ་ཆགས་མ་ཐོགས་པའི་ཡེ་ཤེས་མཐོང་བ་ལ་འཇུག་པ།)

The unshared attributes of Buddhas are so called because Hearers, Solitary Realizers, and ordinary individuals do not possess these qualities. *Being without mistakes* means that beings such as Hearers have faulty actions of body, speech and mind, but the deeds of a Buddha's body, speech and mind are flawless. *Being without mistakes verbally* means that a Hearer shouts to others in a dense forest if he has lost the way, or he will shout, "Who is in there?" into an empty house. This is a result of previous impressions of enjoying meaningless talk. A Buddha does not engage in such speech. *Not decreasing in mindfulness* means that whereas a Hearer engages in awareness of only those factors in his immediate environment, because a Buddha's wisdom has no obstructions or attachment, his mindfulness is without decline. *Not ever not being in meditative equipoise* means that whereas a Hearer can enter into meditative equipoise and then rise from it, a Buddha engages in meditative equipoise at all times and in all activities. Thus a Buddha is never not in meditative equipoise. *Non-discrimination of cyclic existence and nirvana as separate* means that after a Hearer sees the harms of cyclic existence and the virtuous qualities of nirvana, he then discriminates between them. Therefore, he abandons afflictive emotions and practices pure conduct. On the other hand, because a Buddha has great compassion, unmistaken wisdom and an understanding of emptiness, he does not discriminate between cyclic existence and nirvana, which both have the nature of emptiness. *Not being uninterested* means that a Hearer does not take interest in sentient beings' potential for pacification. He does not work for their benefit, and he abandons them. Thus he has a disinterested equanimity. A Buddha, on the other hand, takes interest in sentient beings' potential for pacification. A Buddha has equanimity for those who have no potential because even if he works for their benefit, nothing will be gained. Yet for those who have potential, he does not enter into equanimity and abandon them. Thus he is not disinterested. *Aspiration without decline* means that Hearers do not have the supreme altruistic aspiration to fulfil their own purposes and the purposes of a few other sentient beings. A Buddha has aspiration without decline because he aspires to accomplish the purposes of all sentient beings without exception. *Effort without decline* refers to ever-present awareness of mind and body and the lack of discouragement a Buddha experiences when fulfilling the purpose of even one sentient being who is trying to realize his potential. In this way, a Buddha continually gives teachings. *Mindfulness without decline* is always present within the wisdom of a Buddha who understands the behavior, the thoughts, the unconscious ideas, the mental faculties, the antidotes and the manner of subduing the specific discordant factors of all sentient beings. Hearers do not have this mental capacity. *Wisdom without decline* is the knowledge of 84,000 antidotes to afflictive emotions and the types of behavior that are in accord with these antidotes. Because a Buddha's perfect understanding remains until the purposes of all sentient beings are fulfilled, his wisdom is called wisdom without decline. *Concentration without decline* means that whereas Hearers experience some decline when they enter into meditative equipoise, a Buddha experiences no decline in his meditative equipoise. *Liberation without decline* means that Hearers abide in pacification in which one has only abandoned afflictive emotions. Thus this is an inferior form of liberation. A Buddha has been liberated from both afflictive emotions and obstructions to wisdom. Thus he has attained non-abiding nirvana. Since he remains in the world as long as is necessary to fulfil the purposes of sentient beings, this is called liberation without decline. The *governing of all bodily activities by wisdom* refers to the effortlessness of the deeds of the Buddha even during the period when he was a Bodhisattva. In this period, all of his actions were preceded by deliberation. After attaining enlightenment, his thoughts are unlike a Hearer's; all of his actions are governed by wisdom, and ensue from his initial wisdom. The *governing of all verbal activities by wisdom* refers to the 60 qualities of a Buddha's speech which are in accordance with the minds of sentient beings. These are the result of his previous declaration of all that is required to fulfil the purposes of sentient beings through his wisdom. The *governing of all mental activities by wisdom* refers to the deeds of a Buddha's mind. Having thoroughly abandoned all conceptualization and illusory thought, a Buddha's mind enters into a perception of ultimate reality. His mind penetrates into Dharma spheres, and this is therefore called the governing of all mental activities by wisdom. The *unobstructed wisdom which sees all objects from the past* refers to a Buddha's undeceived understanding of all phenomena which have occurred during previous countless aeons as well as all virtuous and non-virtuous actions of the past. The *unobstructed wisdoms which see all objects from the future and present* are similar to the type of wisdom stated above. A Buddha clearly knows all phenomena which will occur in the future as well as phenomena which exist presently in all directions.

27. THE THREE SETS OF TEACHINGS (སྡེ་སྣོད།)

a. the teachings on moral discipline (འདུལ་བའི་སྡེ་སྣོད།)

b. the teachings on discourses (མདོ་སྡེའི་སྡེ་སྣོད།)

c. the teachings on knowledge (མཛོན་པའི་སྡེ་སྣོད།)

28. THE 12 SCRIPTURAL CATEGORIES (གསུང་རབ་ཡན་ལག)

a. sets of discourses (མདོའི་སྡེ།)

b. intermediate verses (དབྱངས་ཀྱི་བསྙད་པའི་སྡེ།)

c. prophetic teachings (ལུང་དུ་བསྟན་པའི་སྡེ།)

d. verses (ཚིགས་སུ་བཅད་པའི་སྡེ།)

e. specific teachings (ཆེད་དུ་བརྗོད་པའི་སྡེ།)

f. introductory teachings (གླེང་གཞིའི་སྡེ།)

g. parables (རྟོགས་པ་བརྗོད་པའི་སྡེ།)

h. legends (དེ་ལྟ་བུར་བྱུང་བའི་སྡེ།)

i. rebirth stories (སྐྱེ་རབས་ཀྱི་སྡེ།)

j. grand scriptural teachings (ཤིན་ཏུ་རྒྱས་པའི་སྡེ།)

k. marvellous teachings (རྨད་དུ་བྱུང་བའི་སྡེ།)

l. finalized teachings (གཏན་ལ་དབབ་པར་བསྟན་པའི་སྡེ།)

The discourses, intermediate verses, verses, specific teachings, prophetic teachings, grand scriptural teachings and marvellous teachings are all included in the teachings on discourses. The introductory teachings, parables, legends and rebirth stories are all included in the teachings on moral discipline. The finalized teachings are classified as The teachings on knowledge.

29. THE FOUR BASIC INTENTIONS OF BUDDHA FOUND WITHIN THE INTERPRETIVE SUTRAS

(དགོངས་པ།)

a. determining the samenesses (མཉམ་པ་ཉིད་ལ་དགོངས་པ།)

b. determining another period (དུས་གཞན་ལ་དགོངས་པ།)

c. determining another meaning (དོན་གཞན་ལ་དགོངས་པ།)

d. determining the interest of a particular person

(གང་ཟག་གཞན་ལ་དགོངས་པ།)

These intentions refer to a specific method of subduing the minds of sentient beings. Although the original understanding of these words is separate from the meaning attached to them later, there is no contradiction that arises from the words themselves. Therefore these methods are referred to as intentions. *Determining the samenesses* refers to Buddha's statement that he was the previous Buddhas. This is correct because there is no difference in the wisdom body obtained, the amount of merit and wisdom accumulated, or in the number of deeds performed for the sake of sentient beings by the previous Buddhas and Buddha Shakyamuni. The Buddha said that by merely reciting the names of Buddhas such as Amitabha and Avalokiteshvara one will attain enlightenment. However, he did not mean that this would occur immediately. Due to this cause, enlightenment will be obtained eventually. Although the Buddha also said that one will get exactly what one prays for, he did not mean that this would happen immediately. This will happen eventually. Therefore this interpretation is called *determining another period*. The Buddha said that if one does not pay homage to all the Buddhas who are as numerous as the grains of sand on the River Ganges, then one will not understand the present sutra. Yet he did not mean that one would not understand it at the moment it was being told. Rather, at the moment one reaches the first Bodhisattva ground, the sutra will not be clear. Thus this interpretation is called *determining another meaning*. A Buddha gives instructions on those virtuous activities such as ethical conduct for which specific individuals have faith and ability and explains how to enter into their practice. Yet there are those individuals who believe that practicing ethical conduct is all that is necessary. In order to make these people practice the other virtuous activities, he disparages ethical conduct and gives instructions on generosity and so forth. This action of encouraging one to perform all the six perfections is *determining the interest of a particular person*.

30. THE FOUR TYPES OF BUDDHA'S TEACHINGS WHICH REQUIRE INTERPRETATION (ལྡེམ་པོར་དགོངས་པ།)

a. teachings that encourage beings to enter the Mahayana path (ཞུགས་པ་ལ་ལྡེམ་པོར་དགོངས་པ།)

b. teachings on definitions (མཚན་ཉིད་ལ་ལྡེམ་པོར་དགོངས་པ།)

c. teachings on the antidotes (གཉེན་པོ་ལ་ལྡེམ་པོར་དགོངས་པ།)

d. the meanings of the terms used in the teachings (བསྒྱུར་བ་ལ་ལྡེམ་པོར་དགོངས་པ།)

Although these teachings are not of definitive meaning, the Buddha intended them to be interpreted. In this way, he taught in a manner which leads others to enlightenment. Thus these teachings are called the teachings requiring interpretation. For those holding extreme views who questioned whether or not there is an 'I', the Buddha said that there is an 'I' because sentient beings consist of a continual flow of moments. When the Hearers asked if produced objects inherently exist, the Buddha said that the aggregates, sources and constituents all inherently exist because he did not want them to be afraid of the Mahayana teachings and to avoid them. Thus these teachings are the *teachings that encourage beings to enter the Mahayana path*. For those who questioned whether phenomena are produced or not, the Buddha, focusing on the three natures, asserted that phenomena are not produced. This assertion is based upon the nature of imputed phenomena. Buddha also said that phenomena are produced, in which case he was referring to the natures of dependent phenomena and thoroughly established phenomena. Thus these teachings are called the *teachings on definitions*. The reason Buddha taught 84,000 antidotes is because there are 84,000 wrong behaviors. Focusing on the impurities such as attachment, he gave *teachings on the antidotes*. The Buddha taught that one should kill one's father and mother, one should cause division among the religious community, one should kill a Foe Destroyer, and one should draw blood with evil intentions from one who has Gone Thus [a Tathagata]. If one does so, one will reach enlightenment. The meaning of these statements is not exactly as they are stated. Rather, one must kill one's mother, which is ignorance, and one's father, which is hatred. One must refute the inherent existence of the five aggregates with a view of their emptiness, which is dividing the religious order. Recognizing that the mind as the basis-of-all and previous impressions have no inherent existence is killing a Foe Destroyer. The perception through wisdom that all phenomena are empty of inherent existence is the transformation of the term drawing blood from one who has Gone Thus. Furthermore, Buddha taught that that which has no essence has an essence, wrong view abides underneath, and one abandons afflictive emotions with afflictive emotions. In this way, one obtains pure enlightenment. By this he meant that one understands the essence of all phenomena as being emptiness through unwavering meditation, that wrong view abides as the opposite of correct view, and that one abandons the objects of asceticism through ascetic actions. In these ways, one obtains enlightenment. These transformations in meanings are referred to as the *interpretations of the terms used in the teachings*.

31. THE FOUR TRUTHS (བདེན་པ།)

A. SUFFERINGS (སྡུག་བསྔལ་གྱི་བདེན་པ།)

1. impermanence (མི་རྟག་པ།)

2. suffering (སྡུག་བསྔལ་བ།)

3. emptiness (སྟོང་པ།)

4. selflessness (བདག་མེད་པ།)

Impermanence means that regeneration occurs in every instant, which is the nature of death. *Suffering* is either the three sufferings or the eight sufferings, which inflict harm unceasingly. *Emptiness* is the absence of a permanent self abiding in the five aggregates. Those holding extreme views believe in a permanent self. That which those holding extreme views hold to be the self is actually *selfless*.

B. True Causes of Suffering (ཀུན་འབྱུང་གི་བདེན་པ།)

1. origin of all (ཀུན་འབྱུང་།)

2. cause (རྒྱུ།)

3. condition (རྐྱེན།)

4. production (རབ་ཏུ་སྐྱེ་པ།)

The *origin of all* is the abiding within one's continuum of the seeds of rebirth as a being of one of the three realms, through the impressions of afflictive emotions and karma. The virtuous and non-virtuous worldly activities which stem from the afflictive emotions such as desire and hatred are called *causes*. *Conditions* refer to the accumulation of virtuous impressions, which come from virtuous karma, and the accumulation of non-virtuous impressions, which come from non-virtuous karma. The fruits of these eventually mature. *Production* means that after the causes and conditions have come together, one acquires the suffering of the upper or lower realms in accordance with the virtuous or non-virtuous impressions accumulated.

C. True Cessations (འགོག་པའི་བདེན་པ།)

1. cessation (འགོག་པ།)

2. peace (ཞི་བ།)

3. excellence (གྱ་ནོམ་པ།)

4. renunciation (ངེས་པར་འབྱུང་བ།)

Cessation is the abandonment of afflictive emotions such as desire and hatred as well as of non-virtuous actions such as killing. *Peace* means that suffering, which is the result of karma and afflictive emotions, never arises. *Excellence* means that there are no future rebirths within the three realms, and that one never experiences suffering. *Renunciation* means that after one realizes that the three realms are like a prison, one goes to the blissful abode which is beyond sorrow.

D. TRUE PATHS (ལམ་གྱི་བདེན་པ།)

1. path (ལམ།)

2. reason (རིག་པ།)

3. achievement (བསྒྲུབ་པ།)

4. definite freedom (ངེས་པར་འབྱིན་པ།)

The *path* is the way in which one goes from the level of an ordinary individual to the abode of the Aryas. *Reason* is the antidote that abandons the afflictive emotion of ignorance. *Achievement* is the abandonment of wrong views and the accomplishment of the correct view. *Definite freedom* is the freedom from the harms of cyclic existence. One goes to the abode beyond sorrow.

The four truths are to be ascertained in the same order as they are stated. A thorough understanding of true suffering means that one realizes that animate and inanimate objects are the result of the ripening of previous karma. Although one cannot abandon previous karma, one can understand impermanence, suffering, emptiness and selflessness. The abandonment of the true causes of suffering involves the understanding that a rebirth as a being of any of the three realms comes from previous karma and afflictive emotions. Thus a body, which is a heap of suffering, is born. After one sees the way all origins, causes, conditions and production arise, one understands that one can abandon these by following the path. To know true cessation correctly, one realizes that the abandonment of both true suffering and true causes of suffering is the state of nirvana with remainder or the state of nirvana without remainder. One understands that these states are similar to cessation, peace, excellence and renunciation. Next is the way in which one meditates on the path which leads to the cessation of suffering. The path is either the [37] limbs of enlightenment or the eight-fold noble path. Through these actions, one extirpates and abandons suffering and the causes of suffering. Thus one understands path, reason, achievement and definite freedom. When one searches for the selflessness of people and phenomena, one finds them, and one goes from the state of an ordinary being to the state of an Arya.

32. THE FIVE ASPECTS OF THE PATH OF ACCUMU-LATION OF THE HEARERS (ཉན་ཐོས་ཀྱི་ལམ།)

a. the ethical conduct of one who has just entered the path (སོ་སོ་སྐྱེ་ བོའི་ཚུལ་ཁྲིམས།)

b. the restraint of the senses [from objects of attachment] (དབང་པོའི་ སྒོ་བསྡམས་པ།)

c. the restriction of one's food intake (ཟས་ཀྱི་ཚོད་ཤེས་པ།)

d. the refraining from sleep in the evening and the dawn and the enthusiastic practice of yoga during those periods (ནམ་ཀྱི་ཆ་ སྟོད་དང་ཆ་སྨད་ལ་མི་ཉལ་བར་རྣལ་འབྱོར་ལ་བརྩོན་པ།)

e. thorough enjoyment of abiding in introspection (ཤེས་བཞིན་དུ་གནས་ པར་མངོན་པར་དགའ་བ།)

33. THE FOUR LEVELS OF THE PATH OF PREPARATION (རྗེས་པར་འབྱེད་པའི་ཆ།)

a. heat (དྲོད།)

b. peak (རྩེ་མོ།)

c. patience (བཟོད་པ།)

d. supreme worldly Dharma (འཇིག་རྟེན་ཆོས་ཀྱི་མཆོག་)

34. THE 16 MOMENTS OF CONSCIOUSNESS OF THE PATH OF SEEING (མེམས་ཀྱི་རྒྱུ་སྐད་ཅིག་མ།)

a. forbearance with the reality of suffering (སྡུག་བསྔལ་ལ་ཆོས་ཤེས་པའི་ བཟོད་པ།)

b. cognition of the reality of suffering (སྡུག་བསྔལ་ལ་ཆོས་ཤེས་པ།)

c. subsequent forbearance with suffering (སྡུག་བསྔལ་ལ་རྗེས་སུ་རྟོགས་པར་ ཤེས་པའི་བཟོད་པ།)

d. subsequent cognition of suffering (སྡུག་བསྔལ་ལ་རྗེས་སུ་ རྟོགས་པར་ཤེས་པ།)

e. forbearance with the reality of the origin of suffering (ཀུན་འབྱུང་ལ་ ཆོས་ཤེས་པའི་བཟོད་པ།)

f. cognition of the reality of the origin of suffering (ཀུན་འབྱུང་ལ་ཆོས་ ཤེས་པ།)

g. subsequent forbearance with the origin of suffering (ཀུན་འབྱུང་ལ་ རྗེས་སུ་རྟོགས་པས་ཤེས་པའི་བཟོད་པ།)

h. subsequent cognition of the origin of suffering (ཀུན་འབྱུང་ལ་རྗེས་སུ་ རྟོགས་པར་ཤེས་པ།)

i. forbearance with the reality of cessation of suffering (འགོག་པ་ལ་ ཆོས་ཤེས་པའི་བཟོད་པ།)

j. cognition of the reality of the cessation of suffering (འགོག་པ་ལ་ཆོས་ ཤེས་པ།)

k. subsequent forbearance with the cessation of suffering (འགོག་པ་ལ་ རྗེས་སུ་རྟོགས་པར་ཤེས་པའི་བཟོད་པ།)

l. subsequent cognition of the cessation of suffering (འགོག་པ་ལ་རྗེས་སུ་ རྟོགས་པར་ཤེས་པ།)

m. forbearance with the reality of the path (ལམ་ལ་ཆོས་ཤེས་པའི་ བཟོད་པ།)

n. cognition of the reality of the path (ལམ་ལ་ཆོས་ཤེས་པ།)

o. subsequent forbearance with the path (ལམ་ལ་རྗེས་སུ་རྟོགས་པར་ཤེས་ པའི་བཟོད་པ།)

p. subsequent cognition of the path (ལམ་ལ་རྗེས་སུ་རྟོགས་པར་ཤེས་པ།)

35. PATH OF MEDITATION (སྒོམ་པའི་ལམ།)

A. THE SMALL PATH (ལམ་ཆུང་དུ།)
1. the small small (ཆུང་དུའི་ཆུང་དུ།)
2. the small middle (ཆུང་དུའི་འབྲིང་།)
3. the small big (ཆུང་དུའི་ཆེན་པོ།)

B. THE MIDDLE PATH (ལམ་འབྲིང་པོ།)
1. the middle small (འབྲིང་པོའི་ཆུང་དུ།)
2. the middle middle (འབྲིང་པོའི་འབྲིང་པོ།)
3. the middle big (འབྲིང་པོའི་ཆེན་པོ།)

C. THE BIG PATH (ལམ་ཆེན་པོ།)
1. the big small (ཆེན་པོའི་ཆུང་དུ།)
2. the big middle (ཆེན་པོའི་འབྲིང་པོ།)
3. the big big (ཆེན་པོ་ཆེན་པོ།)

D. THE PATH OF PREPARATION (སྦྱོར་བའི་ལམ།)
E. THE PATH WITHOUT OBSTRUCTIONS (བར་ཆད་མེད་པའི་ལམ།)
F. THE PATH OF COMPLETE LIBERATION (རྣམ་པར་གྲོལ་བའི་ལམ།)
G. THE EXTRAORDINARY PATH (ཁྱད་པར་གྱི་ལམ།)

36. THE PATH OF NO MORE LEARNING (མི་སློབ་ལམ།)
This is the path of perfection (མཐར་ཕྱིན་པའི་ལམ།)

37. THE EIGHT LEVELS OF ULTIMATE FREEDOM OF A HEARER (ཉན་ཐོས་ཀྱི་རྣམ་པར་གྲོལ་བའི་ལམ།)

[This path can happen gradually in the stages listed below, or these can all occur simultaneously. The simultaneous fruition of the stages comes after direct insight into the two truths. One then simultaneously abandons all the afflictive emotions that arise from contact with objects in the three realms, by following the transcendental path without obstructions. Thus the fruit of a Stream-enterer and the fruit of a Foe Destroyer occur simultaneously.]

A. THE FOUR TYPES OF APPROACHER (འཇུག་པ།)

1) approacher to the fruit of a Stream-enterer (རྒྱུན་དུ་ཞུགས་པ་ལ་འཇུག་པ།)

2) approacher to the fruit of a Once-returner (ལན་ཅིག་ཕྱིར་འོང་བ་ལ་འཇུག་པ།)

3) approacher to the fruit of a Never-returner (ཕྱིར་མི་འོང་པ་ལ་འཇུག་པ།)

4) approacher to the fruit of a Foe Destroyer (དགྲ་བཅོམ་པ་ལ་འཇུག་པ།)

B. THE FOUR TYPES OF ABIDING (འབྲས་བུ་ལ་གནས་པ།)

1) abider in the fruit of a Stream-enterer (རྒྱུན་དུ་བཞུགས་པའི་འབྲས་བུ་ལ་གནས་པ།)

2) abider in the fruit of a Once-returner (ལན་ཅིག་ཕྱིར་འོང་གི་འབྲས་བུ་ལ་གནས་པ།)

3) abider in the fruit of a Never-returner (ཕྱིར་མི་འོང་པའི་འབྲས་བུ་གནས་པ།)

4) abider in the fruit of a Foe Destroyer (དགྲ་བཅོམ་པའི་འབྲས་བུ་ལ་གནས་པ།)

By abandoning the 88 afflictive emotions of the path of seeing, which is characterized by the 16 moments of wisdom, one attains the position of Stream-enterer. One condenses all four objects of abandonment of the path of meditation, which are the afflictive emotions of the desire realm, into one object. This is then divided into nine (that is, the great-great, great-middle, great-small, and so on, down to small-small). The antidotes of the obstructions to wisdom also have nine corresponding parts. By abandoning the first six of these [obstructions], one obtains the position of a Once-returner. By gradually abandoning all nine, one obtains the position of a Never-returner. Both the form and formless realms have three objects of abandonment condensed into one. There are four concentrations and four formless absorptions. The detailed approach consists of taking the one object of abandonment for each of these eight levels and again dividing it into nine. Through the gradual abandonment of these objects one reaches the peak of cyclic existence. At that point one's afflictive emotions become ever more minute and one's wisdom becomes ever greater. Through the cultivation of vajra-like concentration at this point, one becomes a Foe Destroyer.

38. THE TWO SOLITARY REALIZERS (རང་སངས་རྒྱས།)

[The Solitary Realizer practices the Dharma in accordance with the teachings given to the Hearers. Thus he obtains emancipation from suffering in worldly existence even when no Buddha has appeared.]

A. RHINOCEROS-LIKE SOLITARY REALIZER

(བསེ་རུ་ལྟར་གཅིག་ཏུ་གནས་པ།)

B. SOCIABLE SOLITARY REALIZER (ཚོགས་དང་སྤྱོད་པ།)

39. THE EIGHT MUNDANE PATHS (འཇིག་རྟེན་གྱི་ལམ།)

A. THE FOUR CONCENTRATIONS (བསམ་གཏན།)

[The nature of the subdivisions of the four concentrations is such that they can be placed into one of three categories: antidotes , benefits, or both of these.]

1. The first concentration (བསམ་གཏན་དང་པོ།)
   a. investigation (རྟོག་པ།)
   b. analysis (དཔྱོད་པ།)
   c. joy (དགའ་བ།)
   d. bliss (བདེ་བ།)
   e. single-pointed mind (སེམས་རྩེ་གཅིག་པ་ཉིད།)

2. The second concentration (བསམ་གཏན་གཉིས་པ།)

   a. internal clarity (ནང་རབ་ཏུ་དང་བ།)

   b. joy (དགའ་བ།)

   c. bliss (བདེ་བ།)

   d. single-pointed mind (སེམས་རྩེ་གཅིག་པ་ཉིད།)

3. The third concentration (བསམ་གཏན་གསུམ་པ།)

   a. equanimity (བཏང་སྙོམས།)

   b. mindfulness (དྲན་པ།)

   c. introspection (ཤེས་བཞིན།)

   d. bliss (བདེ་བ།)

   e. single-pointed mind (སེམས་རྩེ་གཅིག་པ་ཉིད།)

4. The fourth concentration (བསམ་གཏན་བཞི་པ།)

a. pure equanimity (བཏང་སྙོམས་ཡོངས་སུ་དག་པ།)

b. pure mindfulness (དྲན་པ་ཡོངས་སུ་དག་པ།)

c. the feeling free from suffering or bliss (སྡུག་བསྔལ་བ་ཡང་མ་ཡིན་བདེ་བ་
ཡང་མ་ཡིན་པའི་ཚོར་བ།)

d. single-pointed mind (སེམས་རྩེ་གཅིག་པ་ཉིད།)

The four concentrations are the four abodes of the form realm. One is not moved by discordant factors at this stage, and one's mental stabilization abides under its own power. The *first concentration* is characterized by investigation and analysis. One understands that making use of sensory stimuli in the desire realm is fault-ridden, like a sickness or scabies. Also, one understands that the four concentrations are pacification and bliss. Thus one acquires these qualities, and one has the joy and bliss that come from the decline of discordant factors. The *second concentration* is characterized by happiness. By way of meditating on the antidotes, joy and bliss arise out of the superior concentration. The *third concentration* is characterized by bliss. If one has happiness, then unhappiness will arise, thus one abandons happiness and therefore one abandons unhappiness as well. Equanimity ensues from this abandonment.

Because one has not abandoned bliss, this stage is bliss. The *fourth concentration* is characterized by equanimity. Since one has bliss on the lower levels, suffering, its counterpart, also arises. Thus one abandons even bliss. Along with this, one abandons even the suffering of breathing in and out. This state is a state of equanimity.

B. THE FOUR FORMLESS ABSORPTIONS (གཟུགས་མེད་པར་འདུག་པ།)

1) the perception of infinite space (ནམ་མཁའ་མཐའ་ཡས་སྐྱེ་མཆེད།)

2) the perception of infinite consciousness (རྣམ་ཤེས་མཐའ་ཡས་སྐྱེ་མཆེད།)

3) the perception of nothingness (ཅི་ཡང་མེད་པ།)

4) the perception that is neither discriminating nor non-
discriminating (འདུ་ཤེས་མེད་འདུ་ཤེས་མེད་མིན་གྱི་སྐྱེ་མཆེད།)

Through the aggregates of feeling, recognition, composite factors and consciousness, one enters into single-pointed meditation on the four formless absorptions. If all phenomena are negated, then there are no longer any produced objects. Everything becomes absorbed by space only, which is infinite. This is the *perception of infinite space*. The *perception of infinite consciousness* comes about when one takes the absorption of infinite space as the object of recognition. Therefore this accompanying consciousness is also infinite. The ensuing aspirational concentration is the perception of infinite consciousness. The *perception of nothingness* comes after one perceives infinite consciousness. One holds the opposite of infinite consciousness as the object of investigation. At that point, one sees neither phenomena with form nor phenomena without form. This results in nothingness. Through aspiration to this and mind stability meditation on this object, one obtains the perception of nothingness. The *perception that is neither discriminating nor non-discriminating* follows the perception of nothingness. One realizes that the discrimination of nothingness is like sickness, scabies and pain. Thus by blocking this discrimination, it becomes more and more subtle. Furthermore, one thinks that if one removes it completely, that as well is inappropriate because it causes fogginess of the mind to arise. Abiding in this subtle discrimination, one engages in a mind stability meditation which is neither a gross discrimination nor a complete absence of discrimination. Thus this is called the perception that is neither discriminating nor non-discriminating.

40. THE EIGHT EMANCIPATIONS (རྣམ་པར་ཐར་པ།)

a. the embodied looking at a form (གཟུགས་ཅན་གཟུགས་ལ་ལྟ་བ།)

b. the discrimination of formlessness looking at a form (ནང་གཟུགས་མེད་པ་འདུ་ཤེས་པས་ཕྱི་རོལ་གྱི་གཟུགས་རྣམས་ལ་ལྟ་བ།)

c. abiding in the accomplishment of the emancipation of a beautiful form (སྡུག་པའི་རྣམ་པ་མངོན་དུ་བྱས་ནས་གནས་པ།)

d. perception of infinite space (ནམ་མཁའ་མཐའ་ཡས་སྐྱེ་མཆེད།)

e. perception of infinite consciousness (རྣམ་ཤེས་མཐའ་ཡས་སྐྱེ་མཆེད།)

f. perception of nothingness (ཅི་ཡང་མེད་པའི་སྐྱེ་མཆེད།)

g. perception that is neither discriminating nor non-discriminating (འདུ་ཤེས་མེད་འདུ་ཤེས་མེད་མིན་གྱི་སྐྱེ་མཆེད།)

h. abiding in the accomplishment of the cessation of discrimination and feeling (འདུ་ཤེས་དང་ཚོར་བ་འགོག་པ་ལུས་ཀྱི་མངོན་སུམ་དུ་བྱས་ནས་གནས་པ།)

The emancipations are the steps one goes through in order to become free from the bonds of afflictive emotions. After one abandons all the afflictive emotions of the path of seeing, one then uses effort to abandon all the objects of abandonment of the path of meditation. The *embodied looking at a form* occurs while one has not yet negated one's own body. However, one refutes inherent existence and permanence by concentrating on the emptiness of inherent existence and impermanence of external forms. The *discrimination of formlessness looking at a form* is the stage where one negates one's own body through the discrimination that it is empty of inherent existence because it is made of parts. Also, one refutes the inherent existence of external forms such as a piece of cloth or a vase through concentration on its emptiness as stated in the first emancipation. *Abiding in the accomplishment of the emancipation of beautiful form* comes after the refutation of inherent existence of one's own body and external forms. At this point, afflictive emotions such as desire do not arise. In order to abolish the generation or non-generation of attachment, one uses one's mind to meditate on the actual nature of beauty. Therefore this is called the emancipation of beautiful form. Abiding in the accomplishment means that one does not generate afflictive emotions such as attachment. One's discriminations go beyond the discrimination of form. At that point, all obstructive discriminations are eradicated. Because the various discriminations of the mind also do not arise, one thinks of this state as limitless space. Thus, having achieved the state of the *perception of infinite space*, one abides in it. After one negates all the objects of eye consciousness such as form, color and shape through an understanding of emptiness, the consciousness, which no longer has an object, does not arise. Also, the accompanying discrimination does not arise. In this way, one's discriminations go beyond the discrimination of form. The objects of the consciousnesses such as ear consciousness, consisting of sound , smell, taste and touch, are also obstructive discriminations, which are negated through an understanding of emptiness. Because these objects do not arise, the consciousnesses which focus on these objects also do not arise. Therefore the accompanying discriminations do not arise. In this way all obstructive discriminations are eradicated. Because these consciousnesses have been eradicated, the ensuing mental consciousness and accompanying mental discriminations also do not arise. Accordingly, because the consciousnesses which perceive and penetrate external objects do not arise, one enters into mind stablity meditation which perceives that all phenomena are absorbed by infinite space. This is the abiding in the perception of infinite space. The *perception of infinite consciousness* surpasses the perception of infinite space. After one's mind moves towards the mind stability meditation on the infinite nature of space which absorbs all phenomena, one thinks that not only is space infinite, but also the discrimination that focuses on infinite space and the accompanying consciousness are infinite like space. Mind stability meditation on this thought is that which surpasses the perception of infinite space. After one achieves this stage of the perception of infinite consciousness, one abides there. *Nothingness* surpasses the perception of infinite consciousness. After one's mind moves towards the perception of infinite consciousness, one focuses on its opposite. After one examines the nature of this, one sees no phenomena, neither those with form nor those without form. Thus one enters into mind stability meditation on this thought, which then surpasses the perception of infinite consciousness. One then abides in the achieved stage of the perception of nothingness. *Perception ·that is neither discriminating nor non-discriminating* surpasses the perception of nothingness. After one's mind moves towards the perception of nothingness one sees it as full of faults, as if it were sickness, scabies or pain. After one extirpates this discrimination, one's discrimination becomes more and more subtle. Yet if one has no discrimination, fogginess of mind arises, and thus this is also an inappropriate state. Thus one abides in a very subtle state of discrimination. Mind stability meditation on this object surpasses the perception of nothingness. One then abides in the achievement of this stage which is the perception that is neither discriminating nor non-discriminating. *Abiding in the accomplishment of the cessation of discrimination and feeling* surpasses the perception that is neither discriminating nor non-discriminating. After one's mind moves towards the perception that is neither discriminating nor non-discriminating, one enters into mind stablity meditation on its cessation. This state surpasses the perception that is neither discriminating nor non-discriminating. At this stage, one extirpates discrimination and its counterparts, the sixth consciousness which is the mental consciousness and the afflicted consciousness. One abides in the cessation of feelings, which all have the nature of suffering, and in the cessation of discrimination, which is like sickness, scabies and pain.

41. THE EIGHT SURPASSING CONCENTRATIONS

(ཟིལ་གྱི་གནོན་པའི་སྐྱེ་མཆེད།)

a. white (དཀར་པོ།)

b. red (དམར་པོ།)

c. yellow (སེར་པོ།)

d. blue (སྔོན་པོ།)

e. attractive (སྡུག་པ།)

f. unattractive (མི་སྡུག་པ།)

g. good (བཟང་པོ།)

h. evil (ངན་པ།)

42. THE NINE MEDITATIVE ABSORPTIONS EXISTING IN SERIES (མཐར་གྱི་གནས་པའི་སྙོམས་པར་འཇུག་པ།)

a. non-conceptuality (མི་རྟོག་པ།)

b. joy (དགའ་བ།)

c. bliss (བདེ་བ།)

d. equanimity (བཏང་སྙོམས།)

e. perception of infinite space (ནམ་མཁའ་མཐའ་ཡས་སྐྱེ་མཆེད།)

f. perception of infinite consciousness (རྣམ་ཤེས་མཐའ་ཡས་སྐྱེ་མཆེད།)

g. perception of nothingness (ཅི་ཡང་མེད་པའི་སྐྱེ་མཆེད།)

h. perception that is neither discriminating nor non-discriminating
(འདུ་ཤེས་མེད་འདུ་ཤེས་མེད་མིན་གྱི་སྐྱེ་མཆེད།)

i. meditative absorption of cessation (འགོག་པའི་སྙོམས་པར་འཇུག་པ།)

The nine meditative absorptions existing in series are the four concentrations, the four formless absorptions, and the cessation of discrimination and feeling. These states are described individually under their respective headings. They are also included under the eight emancipations.

43. THE 10 PERCEPTIONS OF EXHAUSTION
(ཟད་པར་གྱི་སྐྱེ་མཆེད།)

a. the perception of the total pervasion of white (ཟད་པར་དཀར་པོའི་སྐྱེ་མཆེད།)

b. the perception of the total pervasion of red (ཟད་པར་དམར་པོའི་སྐྱེ་མཆེད།)

c. the perception of the total pervasion of yellow (ཟད་པར་སེར་པོའི་སྐྱེ་མཆེད།)

d. the perception of the total pervasion of blue (ཟད་པར་སྔོན་པོའི་སྐྱེ་མཆེད།)

e. the perception of the total pervasion of earth (ཟད་པར་ས་འི་སྐྱེ་མཆེད།)

f. the perception of the total pervasion of water (ཟད་པར་ཆུའི་སྐྱེ་མཆེད།)

g. the perception of the total pervasion of fire (ཟད་པར་མེའི་སྐྱེ་མཆེད།)

h. the perception of the total pervasion of wind (ཟད་པར་རླུང་གི་སྐྱེ་མཆེད།)

i. the perception of the total pervasion of space (ཟད་པར་ནམ་མཁའི་སྐྱེ་ མཆེད།)

j. the perception of the total pervasion of consciousness (ཟད་པར་རྣམ་ པར་ཤེས་པའི་སྐྱེ་མཆེད།)

Some yogis practice the *perception of the exhaustion of earth*. In this way, what is above, below and straight ahead becomes indistinguishable. One's perception of this lack of distinction becomes limitless. Others practice the perception of the *exhaustion of water, fire, wind, blue, yellow, red or white*. In all these cases, what is above, below and straight ahead becomes indistinguishable, and one's perception of this lack of distinction becomes limitless. The yogi who is empowered by this concentration can perceive the exhaustion of whatever he wants. By thinking of any of the four elements, the four colors, space or consciousness, all directions including above and below become only an aggregation of the chosen factor such as fire. Similarly, one has the complete capability to make any of the factors such as colors arise as required. This is the meaning of the perceptions of exhaustion. When one is engaged in this perception of oneness of some factor such as earth or water, then specific, separate phenomena become indistinguishable. This state is limitless because it extends forwards and backwards without limit. One thinks that everything is filled with the chosen factor. One's perception is focused on only this one factor.

44. THE THREE REALMS OF SENTIENT BEINGS (སེམས་ ཅན་གྱི་ཁམས།)

A. THE 20 TYPES OF BEINGS IN THE DESIRE REALM (འདོད་པའི་ཁམས་ན་གནས་པའི་སེམས་ཅན་གྱི་རིས།)

1-8) The eight hot hell realms (ཚ་བའི་དམྱལ་བ།)

a. the eight cold hell realms (གྲང་བའི་དམྱལ་བ།)

b. the trifling hell realms (ཉི་ཚེ་བའི་དམྱལ་བ།)

[These hell realms sometimes only last for a day or two, arising from the karma previously accumulated by an individual. Although the eight cold hell realms and the trifling hell realms are part of the desire realm, only the eight hot hells are considered to be part of this enumeration because they are considered to be the major hell realms.]

9. The animal realm (དུད་འགྲོ།)
[There are those who live in the sea and those who are dispersed among various land masses.]

10. The hungry ghost realm (ཡི་དགས།)
[These beings live in the palace of the ruler of death (gshin rje).]

11-14. The four human continents (མིའི་གླིང་།)

a. using oxen (བ་ལང་སྤྱོད།)

b. unpleasant sound (སྒྲ་མི་སྙན།)

c. great body (ལུས་འཕགས་པོ།)

d. the land of Jambu (འཛམ་བུ་གླིང་།)

15-20. Six types of gods (ལྷའི་རིས།)

a. the land of the four great lineages (རྒྱལ་ཆེན་རིས་བཞི།)

b. the land of the 33 (སུམ་ཅུ་རྩ་གསུམ།)

c. the land without combat (ཐབ་བྲལ།)

d. the joyous land (དགའ་ལྡན།)

e. the land of enjoying emanation (འཕྲུལ་དགའ།)

f. the land of controlling others' emanations (གཞན་འཕྲུལ་དབང་བྱེད།)

B. THE 17 TYPES OF BEINGS IN THE FORM REALM

(གཟུགས་ཁམས།)

1. *The first concentration* (བསམ་གཏན་དང་པོ།)

a. Brahma (ཚངས་པ།)

b. great Brahma (ཚངས་ཆེན།)

c. in front of Brahma (ཚངས་པ་མདུན་ན་འདུན།)

2. *The second concentration* (བསམ་གཏན་གཉིས་པ།)

a. little light (འོད་ཆུང་།)

b. bright light (འོད་ཆེན།)

c. limitless (ཚད་མེད་འོད།)

3. *The third concentration* (བསམ་གཏན་གསུམ་པ།)

a. little virtue (དགེ་ཆུང་།)

b. vast virtue (དགེ་རྒྱས།)

c. limitless virtue (ཚད་མེད་དགེ།)

4. *The fourth concentration* (བསམ་གཏན་བཞི་པ།)

a. cloudless (སྤྲིན་མེད།)

b. born from merit (བསོད་ནམས་སྐྱེས།)

c. great fruit (འབྲས་བུ་ཆེ།)

5. *The five pure places* (གནས་གཙང་མའི་ལྔ།)

a. not great (མི་ཆེ་བ།)

b. without pain (མི་གདུང་བ།)

c. excellent appearance (གྱ་ནོམ་སྣང་བ།)

d. great perception (ཤིན་ཏུ་མཐོང་བ།)

e. below none (འོག་མིན།)

C. THE FOUR DEITIES OF THE FORMLESS REALM

(གཟུགས་མེད་པའི་ཆུའི་རིས།)

1) approaching the perception of infinite space (ནམ་མཁའ་མཐའ་ཡས་ སྐྱེ་མཆེད་དུ་ཉེ་བར་འགྲོ་བ།)

2) approaching the perception of infinite consciousness (རྣམ་ཤེས་ མཐའ་ཡས་སྐྱེ་མཆེད་དུ་ཉེ་བར་འགྲོ་བ།)

3) approaching the perception of nothingness (ཅི་ཡང་མེད་པའི་སྐྱེ་མཆེད་ དུ་ཉེ་བར་འགྲོ་བ།)

4) approaching the perception that is neither discriminating nor non-discriminating (འདུ་ཤེས་མེད་འདུ་ཤེས་མེད་མིན་གྱི་སྐྱེ་མཆེད་དུ་འགྲོ་ བ།)